Praise for *10-Minu...*
for You and You...

Here's another "time-out" book from Grace Fox that is a must for every parent. As usual it's both biblical and practical!

Dr. Gene A. Getz
president, Center for Church Renewal

Grace Fox gets it. She knows kids, and she knows what they need. She has written material that both kids and their parents will love as they learn together how best to honor God and to walk in His ways.

Major Ed Forster
editor in chief, *U.S. War Cry*,
Salvation Army

As a mom, Grace knows that time together with your kids is precious, but devotions had better be short, engaging, funny, and insightful, or your kids will tune out, gripe, or fall asleep. This book will keep your family tuned in, grinning, and wide awake. Better still, the rewards for reading it will be out of this world!

Phil Callaway
speaker and author of *Laughing Matters*
and *Making Life Rich Without Any Money*

For parents who wants to talk about important spiritual issues with their children but don't know how or where to start—this book is for you. Grace Fox combines Scripture, fun stories, and great discussion starters, weaving them together into doable devotion times for parents and kids. Not only will children benefit, but moms and dads will grow spiritually too!

Glynnis Whitwer
author and senior editor,
Proverbs 31 Ministries

Who says family devotions have to be boring? Time-outs with your children can be positive, productive, and fun as you reinforce biblical principles and show your kids how to live godly lives in today's challenging world.

David and Claudia Arp
authors of *10 Great Dates* and
The Connected Family

10-Minute Time Outs for You and Your Kids is an invitation for families to experience the life-changing benefits of storytelling, sharing faith experiences, and enjoying family prayer. It's from this sacred place that memories are formed and a legacy is passed on. Grace Fox has written another winner!

Margaret Gibb
president of Women Alive

10-Minute Time Outs for You and Your Kids is a treasure chest packed with practical nuggets of wisdom for kids! I only wish Grace's book was around when I was running family devotions for *my* kids! But praise God, I will have it on the shelf for my grandchildren!

Pam Farrel
author of *10 Best Decisions a Parent Can Make*
and coauthor of *Got Teens?*

Looking for devotionals that your children will love and not think boring? Look no further! Grace captures the heart of a child with real-life, engaging, winsome stories that lead them to love the Word and desire to be like Jesus.

Fern Nichols
founder of Moms in Touch International

My 12-year-old son and I sat down to read one of the devotions from *10-Minute Time Outs for You and Your Kids*. We loved them so much we read three! We laughed out loud, prayed together, and talked about how wonderful God is. Nathan said, "The stories are great, and I learned a lot about God. It was like going on a treasure hunt and finding gold." How can a mom not love that? We've already set a date for a 10-minute time out tomorrow!

Tricia Goyer
author of *Generation NeXt Parenting*
and *Life Interrupted: The Scoop
on Being a Young Mom*

10-Minute Time Outs for You and Your Kids is the answer to a parent's struggle to provide quality spiritual time together even with a busy lifestyle. These quick, power-packed, contemporary devotions deal with current issues for 8- to12-year-olds. They infuse the power of God's Word and show how to face daily challenges by making godly choices.

Annetta E. Dellinger
author of *Happy Talk* and
Adopted and Loved Forever

10-Minute Time Outs

FOR You & Your Kids

Scriptures, Stories, *and* Prayers You Can Share Together

GRACE FOX

HARVEST HOUSE PUBLISHERS

EUGENE, OREGON

Cover by Koechel Peterson & Associates, Inc.

Cover photo © Tom Henry/Koechel Peterson & Associates

10-MINUTE TIME OUTS FOR YOU AND YOUR KIDS
Copyright © 2007 by Grace Fox
Published by Harvest House Publishers
Eugene, Oregon 97402
www.harvesthousepublishers.com

Library of Congress Cataloging-in-Publication Data
Fox, Grace, 1958–
 10-minute time outs for you and your kids / Grace Fox.
  p. cm.
 ISBN 978-0-7369-1860-2 (pbk.)
 1. Family—Prayer-books and devotions—English. 2. Family—Religious life I. Title. II. Title:
Ten minute time outs for you and your kids.
 BV4526.3.F69 2007
 249—dc22
                                    2006021719

Printed in the United States of America

09 10 11 12 13 14 15 / LB-CF / 10 9 8 7 6 5 4 3

Acknowledgments

As always, I owe my deepest thanks to my husband, Gene. I couldn't have written this manuscript without your practical support. Thank you for cooking and for washing the dinner dishes so I could finish each day's project. Thank you for locating the perfect laptop so I could continue writing when speaking engagements took me far from my office. Thanks for praying for me and with me throughout the writing and editing process. I could go on and on, but I have a page limit. I love you.

Thanks to my children—Matthew, Stephanie, Kim, and my beautiful daughter-in-love, Cheryl. Your faith in God blesses me. Your trust in His ability to provide finances for college challenges me to trust Him more. Your desire to serve Him wherever He leads excites me. I know God has big things in store for you!

Thanks to my agent, Wendy Lawton. You're a wise business woman, but you're also my friend and prayer partner. Thank you for listening when I share my dreams and for helping bring them into reality.

Thanks to my Harvest House family. Your willingness to partner with me has resulted in countless lives being encouraged and changed. Eternity will tell the results of your behind-the-scenes effort.

Thanks to my prayer team. I'm humbled by your willingness to read my monthly e-mails and hold me up before the Lord. Your prayers give me the strength, creativity, and focus I need to complete these projects. May God bless you more than you could ever imagine!

Thanks to my parents, Henry and Susan, and my in-laws, Tim and Betty. You've given me the privilege of a godly heritage—a treasure money can't buy.

And most importantly, thanks to God. You are my everything. I place this book in Your hands and trust You to use it for Your highest purpose. I pray that its truths will teach the next generation how to light up the darkness. And may children and parents alike fall on their knees in worship before You. You deserve it!

Those who are wise will shine as bright as the sky, and those who turn many to righteousness will shine like stars forever.
DANIEL 12:3

A Note from the Author

Dear Parents,

You deserve a gold medal for investing in your family's spiritual well-being! Raising your children to become God-fearing young men and women is the most important task you'll ever have. Why? Because God desires a relationship with them. He has a unique purpose for each one. And when they know Him and follow His ways, they will possess the power to impact our nation for good and, ultimately, for God. Heaven knows our society needs their influence.

Your task is a challenging one. Media bombard today's kids with messages that stray far from the truth. "Explore and appreciate your own reality," they imply. "So long as you honor your hearts, you can do whatever pleases you."

Sadly, that philosophy has infiltrated the Christian community. The host of a well-known radio program recently stated that only one in ten Christian young people believe in absolute truth. *One in ten!* That figure astounds and sobers me. It also makes me want to stand up and shout, "It's time to turn this around! God has called His people to shine as lights in the world! If we want to illumine the darkness, we must embrace the attitudes and actions that set us apart as His people!" And *that's* why I've written this book.

My desire is that the devotions within its pages will help you teach your kids basic principles regarding how to honor God and walk in His ways. I'll be the happiest author alive if it influences your kids to become doers of the Word and to obey God with deep reverence and fear (Philippians 2:12). I'll be thrilled beyond measure if they learn that God works within them and empowers them to do what pleases Him (verse 13). And I will fall on my face in thanksgiving if its truths encourage them to live clean, innocent lives as children of

God, shining as lights in a dark world full of crooked and perverse people (verse 15).

God's Word teaches us everything we need to know about shining as lights in today's society. It's a treasure chest overflowing with pearls of wisdom and gems of truth. When we seek and apply its principles, they reward us with eternal wealth beyond our wildest imaginations.

I've formatted *10-Minute Time Outs for You and Your Kids* with the treasure-chest analogy in mind. Each devotion requires only a few minutes and follows a simple format using the treasure theme:

- Read the Clue—a key verse for the day
- Discover the Treasure—a story and application
- Share the Wealth—a Scripture-based prayer and discussion question
- Hide a Jewel—a memory verse that reinforces the day's theme

As you use this book, rest assured that I'm praying for you and your family. Having raised a son and two daughters, I understand your desire for your family's spiritual well-being and can relate to your concerns and fears in that regard. I also know that your efforts are worth every minute, so keep them a priority in the midst of your busy life.

I've walked the road you're traveling now, and I'm cheering you on!

Know you are loved,

Grace
www.gracefox.com

A Great Big Wonderful God!

Read the Clue

> For God made two great lights, the sun and the moon, to shine down upon the earth. The greater one, the sun, presides during the day; the lesser one, the moon, presides through the night. He also made the stars (Genesis 1:16).

Discover the Treasure

Shortly after midnight, Jason and his friend Mike spread their sleeping bags on the lawn and crawled inside. They felt tired, but they refused to sleep. Instead, they studied the night sky for a predicted meteor shower.

"We're in for a good show," said Mike. "The TV weatherman said we might see a train."

"A *what?*" asked Jason.

"A train. It's a long, glowing tail behind a meteor."

The boys gazed at the stars twinkling like tiny diamonds against the black velvet sky. Mike broke the silence after several minutes. "Do you know what I read in a science book? I read that stars are giant balls of glowing gas. The sky's full of them! There are more than 200 billion billion."

Jason reached for his backpack and pulled out a paper, pencil, and flashlight. He scribbled some numbers, stopped to count, and then added a few more digits. He looked at the number on the page—200, 000,000,000,000,000,000—and whistled. "That's a lot of zeroes! I can't even imagine that many stars."

"Me neither," said Mike. "But that's not all. Did you know that the sun is the closest star to the earth? The next nearest star is so far from us that the fastest jet would take a million years to fly there."

"Wow! That's amazing," said Jason. "What else did the book say?"

"Some stars are a thousand times bigger than the sun. They're called supergiants." Mike paused for a moment and then said, "You know what? Someday I'd like to be an astronomer. I think I'd enjoy studying the stars and galaxies and black holes and all that stuff. I'd like to know how they got there and what keeps them from falling from the sky."

"I know how they got there," said Jason. "God put them there. Your science book probably didn't say that, but the Bible says it's true."

"Yeah?" said Mike. Now it was his turn to ask the same question Jason had asked a few moments earlier. "What else does that book say?"

"My Sunday school teacher read a verse about stars last week. It said that God decides the number of stars in the sky, and He calls them all by name. Can you imagine naming 200 billion billion stars and remembering each one? That thought boggles my mind."

That thought boggles my mind too. In fact, my imagination can't begin to comprehend how enormous the universe is. And God is even bigger!

Some people think God can fit in a pocket or on a shelf. They whittle a shape from wood, place it on a windowsill, and pray to it. Some folks think God lives in a stone or in a tree.

But God isn't like that. He's big! He's incredible! And He's alive! He made and named the stars. He created everything else in nature too. He's so amazing that our imaginations have a hard time stretching far enough to understand Him.

Because God is so great, He deserves our love and admiration. He's pleased when we tell Him that we trust Him. He can't be stuffed in a pocket or set on a bookshelf. He's bigger than the universe, and He alone deserves our worship.

Share the Wealth

We praise You, God, for being the Creator of the sun, moon, and stars (Genesis 1:16). You are great and mighty in power, and Your understanding has no limit (Psalm 147:5). Because You are so great and mighty, You can be trusted. Please help us trust You more and more every day. Amen.

Lie outside on a clear night and study the sky. Find the Little Dipper and Big Dipper. Search the sky for Sirius, the brightest star. It's more than 20 times brighter than the sun and more than twice its size. Astronomers have nicknamed it *Dog Star* because it is located in the eye of the Canis Major constellation.

Hide a Jewel

He determines the number of the stars and calls them each by name. Great is our Lord and mighty in power; his understanding has no limit (Psalm 147:4-5 NIV).

Idol Worship

Read the Clue

Do not make idols or set up carved images, sacred pillars, or shaped stones to be worshiped in your land. I, the LORD, am your God (Leviticus 26:1).

Discover the Treasure

"Carl, it's time to eat dinner," said Mom. "Can you please take your baseball cards off the kitchen table?"

Carl glanced from the rows of carefully arranged cards to his mom and back again. "Do I have to? I spent nearly a half hour lining them up."

Mom shook her head. "Sorry. I realize that. But I also realize you've claimed the kitchen table to admire your cards just before dinner three times this week. I'm sure we can find a better plan. For now, though, it's time to move them."

Carl groaned and boxed his cards. He carried the box to his bedroom and placed it on his dresser between his baseball mitt and an autographed picture of his favorite major-league player, and then he returned to the kitchen.

"By the way," said Mom, "we're hoping to visit Grandma and Grandpa this weekend. We haven't seen them for a couple of months—our visit is long overdue."

"I can't go," stated Carl. "I have plans."

Mom stopped tossing the salad and faced Carl. "Oh, really?"

"Yep. I'm playing ball with my friends on Saturday afternoon. On Sunday, I want to watch the ball tournament at the community center. Maybe a team will need a water boy. You'll have to go without me. I can probably stay at Joe's place."

Mom paused for a moment while she thought about her response. Then she said quietly, "Grandma and Grandpa haven't been feeling well lately. I know they want to see you."

"Oh well." Carl shrugged. "It won't happen this weekend."

"Sit down, Son," said Mom. She pulled out a chair and seated herself. "It seems you have only one thing on your mind—baseball."

"That's because I love baseball. Is that wrong?" said Carl. "Sheesh— it's only ball. It could be *girls* or something."

Mom smiled. "I understand. There's nothing wrong with baseball itself. But I'm concerned when it consumes your thoughts day and night and when it causes you to overlook your grandparents' needs. Do you remember the missionaries at church last Sunday?"

Carl nodded.

"Do you remember what they spoke about?"

"They talked about seeing people worship idols."

"That's right. They said they've seen people worship idols made of rock and wood and metals such as bronze and gold. We don't see that form of idol worship happen here, but we often see it happen in a different way."

"What do you mean?"

"Idols are simply anything that we love and worship more than God. In this case, it seems that baseball is an idol. It's consuming your thoughts and time, and it's causing you not to care about other people."

Carl fidgeted with the tablecloth. "I never thought about it like that. I don't want to worship idols no matter what they look like."

"Then perhaps you'll want to reconsider your weekend plans," said Mom.

"I will."

As Carl's mom said, nothing is wrong with baseball. It's a fun game to watch and play. Nothing is wrong with buying name-brand clothes or fancy computer systems or with being a great athlete or wanting to look pretty either. But when anything becomes more important than God or the people He loves, we run into trouble. That trouble is called idol worship.

God's Word tells us to worship only the true God. He wants us to love Him more than anything. More than awards for good grades, more than our friends, more than our favorite video game. More than *anything*. When we do that, our focus stays in the right place, and we act the way He wants us to. We show that we trust Him, and not nice things or accomplishments, to help us through life (Psalm 115:2-9).

Share the Wealth

> Dear Father, thank You for giving us good things to enjoy
> in life. Thank You too for warning us not to be greedy for
> them because that's idolatry (Colossians 3:5). Help us love
> You more than anything else in the world. Amen.

Read Psalm 115:9: "O Israel, trust the LORD! He is your helper; he is your shield." Now read Psalm 96:5-6: "The gods of other nations are merely idols, but the LORD made the heavens. Honor and majesty surround him. Strength and beauty are in his sanctuary." From these verses, tell several reasons why God alone deserves our worship.

Hide a Jewel

> *Dear children, keep away from anything that might take*
> *God's place in your hearts* (1 John 5:21).

No Fear

Read the Clue

Who else has held the oceans in his hand? Who has measured off the heavens with his fingers? Who else knows the weight of the earth or has weighed out the mountains and the hills? (Isaiah 40:12).

Discover the Treasure

In October, 1996, our family moved to an island in British Columbia, Canada. Before long, we discovered that island dwelling brings unique adventures.

Eleven days after we moved, a local family invited us to join them on their homeschool field trip. The mother had arranged to visit a courthouse and a police station in the nearest city. Getting there meant riding a ferry across the Inside Passage—the marine highway for tugboats and cruise ships traveling to and from Alaska.

The ten-minute ride is beautiful on warm summer days. People often leave their vehicles and climb the stairs to the ferry's upper decks, where they bask in the sunshine and enjoy the scenery. But stormy fall and winter days are a different story. Wind and waves cause the ferry to shudder and rock from side to side. Whitecaps splash over the ferry's walls, and saltwater sprays the cars and trucks.

We'd hoped that sunshine would wake us on the morning of our field trip. Instead, howling wind and pounding rain shook us from our sleep. Minutes after we boarded the ferry, it left the sheltered harbor and entered the choppy water.

My kids and I tried to fake courage, but our wide eyes betrayed us. "Don't worry," said the other mother. "We'll be fine, but the ferry might shut down if the storm continues. We should have brought our pajamas in case we can't get home tonight."

The ferry continued rocking and rolling its way across the channel. *O God,* I prayed silently, *Please, p-l-e-a-s-e keep us safe.*

When I prayed, God calmed my fears. He reminded me that He made the oceans. In fact, He reminded me that He holds the oceans in His hands! And He assured me that since He could do that, He was certainly able to carry our ferry safely to the other side.

Sure enough, several minutes later, the ferry reached its destination, and we drove onto dry land. The storm stopped the ship from running for the next 11 hours, and we didn't arrive back home until nearly midnight, but that was okay because the field trip was a huge success. We learned a lot about the courthouse and police station, and we also learned an important life lesson: God wants us to trust Him when we feel afraid.

Have you ever felt frightened, the way my family and I did during the storm? Perhaps a bad dream wakes you at night and makes you want to hide under your covers. Or a bully at school threatens to hurt you, and you're afraid that others might think you're a wimp if you don't fight back. Maybe you're having a difficult time understanding a subject at school, and you're afraid of failing a test. Or a grandparent is sick, and you worry that he'll never be well again.

We all feel afraid at times. When it happens, we can remember that God is B-I-G. He holds the oceans in His hands. He measures the heavens with His fingers. And He weighs the mountains and hills in a scale. He's bigger than any thing or person that causes us to feel afraid, and He can help us in every situation.

Share the Wealth

God, You are amazing. Holding the oceans in our hands is impossible, but You can do it easily. We can only guess how big the universe is, but You can measure it with Your fingers. Scientists calculate the weight of the earth, but You've known it all along. We can't put the mountains and hills in a scale, but You can do it all (Isaiah 40:12). When we feel afraid, remind us that Your right hand holds us, and You will help us (Isaiah 41:13). Amen.

What makes you feel afraid? Tell God, "I'm glad You're bigger than _____ (fill in the blank with your answer to the question). I'm thankful that You can help me when I feel afraid."

Hide a Jewel

I am holding you by your right hand—I, the LORD your God. And I say to you, "Do not be afraid. I am here to help you" (Isaiah 41:13).

The Flashlights

Read the Clue

Send out your light and your truth; let them guide me. Let them lead me to your holy mountain, to the place where you live (Psalm 43:3).

Discover the Treasure

James and his friends wanted to do something fun during their school's winter break. "Let's take a hike," said James. "I know about a park trail that leads to a great viewpoint. I walked it last summer. The trip up and back takes about three hours. Want to go?" The other fellows nodded.

James' father offered to drop off the boys at the head of the trail after lunch that day. "I'll be back by 4:30," he said. "Here—take these flashlights." He handed them a bag containing four lights. "Darkness comes early these days, especially when you're surrounded by tall trees. I don't want anyone getting lost."

The boys waved goodbye and began their trek. The path wound through ferns and towering fir trees. Halfway up the slope, James stopped to catch his breath. "I don't feel like carrying this bag," he said. "We won't need these flashlights anyway. I'll leave them here, and we can pick them up on the way back."

Up, up, up, the trail climbed, leading the group to a clearing from

16

which they could see surrounding hills and towns for miles. They sat on a boulder and devoured granola bars as they surveyed the scenery.

Suddenly one boy had an idea. "Have you heard about *cairns?*"

"Never," said James. "What are they?"

"They're piles of rocks. People stack them like a monument to mark a special place. Let's make one."

The group scoured the clearing for rocks. They heaped their finds in a mound and shoved a stick in the top for extra flourish. More than an hour after reaching the summit, James glanced at his watch. "Oh-oh, it's nearly four o'clock. Dad will be in the parking lot at 4:30, and we haven't started back yet."

The boys grabbed their packs and began their hike. The path was slippery, making their descent slower than they'd expected. The afternoon sunshine faded. Before long, inky blackness enveloped them. "I can barely see the trail," said James. "Leaving those flashlights behind wasn't such a smart idea after all. Maybe we should stop and wait for help."

"No way," one voice said. "What if help doesn't come? I don't want to spend the night out here."

The group pressed forward at a snail's pace, their feet snapping twigs and snagging on ivy. The underbrush grew thicker with each step, and prickly bushes caught on the kids' jackets.

"Something's wrong," said James. "I think we're off the path. We'd better holler for help. Maybe someone will hear us." And holler they did—"Help! Help! Is anyone there?"

A familiar voice responded: "Boys—I'll find you! Stay where you are. Just yell again—I'll follow your voices!"

Moments later, the boys caught sight of a light beam bobbing between the trees. "Dad! Over here!" called James. The beam came closer and stopped about 15 feet below the group. "Up here, Dad!" The light scanned the forest and finally rested on the lost hikers.

"Yikes! What are you doing up there?" asked James' dad. "The path is down here." He bushwhacked up the slope and joined the boys.

"Boy, are we glad to see you!" said James. The others agreed.

"I'm glad to see you too," said his dad. "Hey—you'll never guess what I found on my way up here." He held up the bag containing the flashlights. "What's with this?"

"I'm sorry," said James. "I set them down because I didn't feel like carrying the bag, and besides, I didn't think we'd need them. I was wrong."

"Wrong indeed," said his dad. He pulled out the flashlights and handed one to each boy. "Without these, you'll likely stumble in the darkness all night. But if you use them as they're intended, you'll find your way. Ready?"

"Ready." The boys clicked on their flashlights and lit up the darkness. "Let's go."

Did you know that God's Word is like a light? Just as the flashlights lit up the forest path and enabled James and his friends to return safely to the parking lot, so God's Word lights up our path through life.

Sometimes we face frightening situations. We feel lost and don't know what to do. But God's Word is like a light—it shines in our darkness by reminding us not to be afraid because God is with us at all times and everywhere we go (Joshua 1:9). Sometimes we face problems that frustrate or confuse us. God's Word lights up the darkness by reminding us that the Lord gives wisdom when we ask for it (James 1:5). The Bible is the light that shows us the answers to life's problems. When we read and obey it, it shows us how to live and keeps us on track.

Share the Wealth

Dear God, thank You for giving us the Bible. Thank You that it's a lamp for our feet, teaching us how to walk through life. Thank You that it's a light for our path, showing us the way to go (Psalm 119:105). Help us remember that it's the light that will keep us safe. Amen.

Parents, recall an incident where God's Word was a light to your path. Tell the story to your children.

Hide a Jewel

Your word is a lamp for my feet and a light for my path (Psalm 119:105).

Wise Guy

Read the Clue

Give me an understanding mind so that I can govern your people well and know the difference between right and wrong (1 Kings 3:9).

Discover the Treasure

Friday afternoon—the end of another school week. The bell rang, doors flung open, and students spilled into the hallway. Excited chatter filled the air as the kids found their lockers and gathered their belongings.

Within minutes only five boys remained in the hall. Four huddled and whispered, casting glances at the fifth—Mark, the new kid in school—as he stuffed his binder and textbooks into his backpack.

Mark's family had moved to that town only two weeks prior. His dad's job transfer had meant leaving his buddies and soccer team behind. It meant having no one to hang out with after school and on weekends until he made new friends, and that thought didn't exactly thrill him. Striking up conversations with strangers was far beyond his comfort zone. But today, as he faced his third lonely weekend since the move, he was ready to do almost anything to find friends.

Mark closed his locker and walked toward the exit. That's when he heard his name.

"Hey, Mark," said Rick, the group's leader. "Do you have plans for tonight?"

Mark stopped. "Not yet," he said.

"We do. Wanna join us?"

"Sure. Why not?"

Rick gave instructions. "You know the abandoned house that's five blocks north of here?" Mark nodded. "Meet us there at seven o'clock."

Three hours later, Mark met the boys behind the shack. He'd anticipated a hike or a bike ride, but he instantly knew they intended otherwise.

"Hey, Mark, look at this!" said Rick. The boys unzipped their backpacks and pulled out several packages of cigarettes and five bottles of beer. They laughed as they swapped stories about stealing the stash from their parents' supply.

Mark stared. Stolen cigarettes and beer? Sure, he wanted friends, but he wasn't *that* desperate.

"Here, have some," said Rick. He offered Mark a beer and a smoke.

Mark shook his head. "No, thanks. In fact, I think I have plans after all." He turned to leave.

"Too bad. You lose," said Rick as he put a cigarette to his lips and lit a match.

Later that evening, Mark told his dad about what happened. "I'm proud of you, Son," said his father. "Your decision showed wisdom. Do you know what that is?"

"Not exactly," said Mark.

"Having wisdom means knowing the difference between right and wrong. Every morning I pray that you'll grow in wisdom, just as Jesus did when He was a boy. God is answering my prayers—you recognized the boys' activities as being wrong. By refusing to participate, you chose what's right. God will bless your decision because He values wisdom. He wants you to make choices that please Him."

"Thanks for your prayers," said Mark, "but maybe you could pray about something else while you're at it. I'd really appreciate having friends to hang out with. And I'd like to do something fun tomorrow."

"We can fix that," said his dad. "Let's go fishing. If you like, we can invite Rick and the other boys. Perhaps we can show them they don't need beer and cigarettes to have fun."

God's Word says wisdom is important. Solomon's story proves it. This young man became the king of Israel when his father, King David, died. Before long, God appeared to Solomon in a dream and said he could ask for anything he wanted. Solomon could have asked for lots of money or a fancy palace or more livestock or servants than he already had. Instead, he asked for wisdom because he wanted to be a good king for his people (1 Kings 3:5-9). God was so pleased with Solomon's request that He made him the wisest person who ever lived (1 Kings 3:12).

Being wise is more important than being pretty or owning fun stuff or being popular. That's because wisdom helps us make good choices, and wise choices are important for living in a way that pleases God.

Share the Wealth

Dear God, we praise You because You alone have all wisdom and power (Daniel 2:20). Thank You for promising to give wisdom when we ask for it (James 1:5). Thank You for loving us enough to give us everything we need to live in a way that pleases You. Amen.

Read 1 Kings 3:16-28. How did Solomon show wisdom in the situation with the two women and one baby?

Hide a Jewel

If you need wisdom—if you want to know what God wants you to do—ask him, and he will gladly tell you. He will not resent your asking (James 1:5).

Just Say No

Read the Clue

But when the Holy Spirit controls our lives, he will produce this kind of fruit in us: love, joy, peace, patience, kindness, goodness, faithfulness, gentleness, and self-control (Galatians 5:22-23).

Discover the Treasure

"How does *this* look?" asked Amy as she stepped from the dressing room. She modeled a pair of black corduroy pants and a lime green turtleneck sweater for her friend Suzanne.

"Looks great!" said Suzanne. "So did the other two outfits you tried on. I think you should buy them all."

"I don't think so," said Amy. "I can only afford one."

"That's no fun," said Suzanne. "You have a debit card, don't you? You've been saving money from birthday checks and babysitting jobs. You must have enough money to pay for them."

"I *do* have enough money, but that's not the point," said Amy. She twirled before the mirror, examining her appearance from every angle.

"So what is the point?"

"I don't need three new outfits," Amy explained. She stopped twirling and leaned against the door frame. "I have other clothes in my closet. Why should I add more to that collection? Besides, I'm saving money for a summer missions trip with my youth group. If I spend it all on clothes, I won't have enough for the trip."

"C'mon, just buy them," coaxed Suzanne.

Amy put her hands on her hips and cast a fake glare at her friend. "You're not listening to me. Have you forgotten what happened last year?"

Suzanne grinned sheepishly. She recalled her first major mall adventure without her mom. She bought lots of cute clothes on sale. Then she added a new purse, some eye shadow, and a few other odds and ends—nothing she really needed, just stuff that seemed cool at the time. The problem was, her out-of-control spending drained her bank account.

When Suzanne's friends attended a carnival a week later, she had to stay home because she couldn't afford a ticket. When they invited her to a concert, she couldn't go. When her favorite musical group released a new CD, she couldn't buy it. She'd begged her folks for a few dollars, but they shook their heads. They said, "We've tried to teach you about controlling your spending habits, but you haven't listened. Sorry." It had been a long summer and not much fun.

"You're right," said Suzanne. "I needed the reminder. Self-control— learning to control my desires and actions. Gotcha. So, if you're only buying one outfit, which one will you choose?"

Amy has learned self-control. She controls her desires and spends money only on her needs rather than on her wants. By doing so, she'll enjoy the benefit of saving her money for something more worthwhile—participating on her youth group's summer missions trip.

Suzanne is still learning. Even as a young girl, she spent money on things that she wanted but didn't really need—candy, stick-on tattoos, and other such stuff. Her parents tried to teach her the importance of controlling her desires and her spending habits, but she refused to listen. She learned the hard way. Ouch.

Practicing self-control when we spend money is important, but it's important in other areas of life too. For example, we must learn to control our temper. We might want to smack someone or yell hurtful words when we're angry, but self-control helps us show respect instead. We might want to whine or complain about a grade we feel is unfair, but self-control enables us to talk politely with the teacher. Self-control even applies to our eating habits. We may feel like eating chocolate cake and ice cream three times a day, but self-control helps us say no.

God knows that controlling our desires is often difficult and that failing to do so can sometimes hurt us. Because He loves us and wants to protect us from the consequences of bad choices, He sent His Holy Spirit to help us. He lives in those who love God, and He gives us the strength to say no to our desires and yes to right behavior. When our lives show self-control, others know that we belong to God, and He is pleased.

Share the Wealth

Dear God, thank You for sending Your Holy Spirit to live in us and teach us self-control. Please give us the strength to say no to desires that would carry bad consequences (Galatians 5:22-23) and help us live in a way that makes You smile. We love You. Amen.

In what area of your life do you need to learn self-control? Here are some examples:

- the words you speak when you feel angry
- the amount of time you spend playing computer games or watching television every day
- choosing good books to read versus books that pollute your mind and heart
- the foods you eat
- the attitude you show when you play competitive sports

Hide a Jewel

It is better to be patient than powerful; it is better to have self-control than to conquer a city (Proverbs 16:32).

Play by the Rules

Read the Clue

Loving God means keeping his commandments, and really, that isn't difficult. For every child of God defeats this evil world by trusting Christ to give the victory (1 John 5:3-4).

Discover the Treasure

Sara dashed across her family's front lawn and headed for the neighbor's home, where she would spend the evening babysitting. Three little faces grinned at her through the living room window as she approached. *I wonder how they'll behave tonight?* she thought as she waved at the six-year-old triplets. Babysitting in that household was never dull. The kids—one girl and two boys—bopped from one adventure to another, fueled by wild imaginations.

The parents gave final instructions and kissed their kids goodbye. After they'd driven away, Sara turned to the trio. "So, what would you like to do?"

"Play a game!" shouted the girl. "We have a new one." She ran to a closet and pulled out a board game. She plopped the box on the kitchen table and dumped out its contents. Her brothers climbed onto nearby chairs and helped arrange the pieces as Sara read the rules aloud.

"Each player rolls two dice. One has colored spots—green, red, and blue. The other has black dots. One side has one dot, another has two, another has three....all the way to six. See?" Sara rotated the dice to show the children. "If one dice rolls green and the other rolls three, for example, you move forward three spaces. If the colored dice rolls blue and the other rolls a four, you move backward four spaces. If one dice rolls red, you can't move. Let's play a practice round."

The girl rolled her dice first. "A green spot and two dots," she said. She picked up her game piece and moved it forward two spaces.

"You can't do that!" objected one brother. "You have to move backward."

"No, I don't!" his sister argued. "The rules say I move ahead."

"Backward!" her brother said. He grabbed the game piece and moved it back. Then he stuck his face close to hers and stared into her eyes. "I don't care what those rules say. I made up my own."

That's when Sara became the referee. "Whoa—wait a minute," she said. "The person who created this game wants us to enjoy it. The rules are there for a purpose. If we toss them out and make up our own, we get confused. Worse yet, we ruin all the fun."

"Sara's right," said the girl. "Play by the rules! Don't make up your own!"

"Oh, all right," said her brother. "Go ahead. Move your player ahead."

Rules, rules, rules. Life is full of rules, and obeying them is important. For instance, imagine what might happen if...

- A car driver said, "Stopping for red lights is silly. I think I'll ignore that rule."
- A pedestrian said, "Crosswalks are made to help me cross the road safely, but I don't want to use them. I'll ignore that rule."
- A child said, "Mom told me not to touch the hot stove element, but I'm not going to obey her."

Safety rules are important, but we have other important rules to follow—those found in the Bible. For instance, one rule tells us not to steal. We're headed for trouble if we say, "That's a stupid rule. I don't have enough money to buy the video game I really want. Taking it when the store clerk isn't looking is the only way to get it." Stealing ruins everything—it makes us feel guilty, keeps others from trusting us, and leads to trouble with the law.

Another God-given rule is to speak the truth. Tossing out that rule and telling lies leads to problems. Before long, we're telling more lies to cover up those we've already told! And, again, people will learn that they can't trust us.

God is wiser than anyone else. He knows how we can best enjoy life, so He gives rules to help make that possible. His rules are not meant to make our lives miserable; they're for our benefit. We win when we follow them. We lose when we don't. What would you rather be—a loser or a winner?

Share the Wealth

> Dear God, thank You for delighting in those who obey Your commands. Please help us obey You. Teach us to turn to You with all our heart and soul (Deuteronomy 30:20). Amen.

Telling the truth and not stealing are two rules God has given us in His Word. List three others. Why are those rules important?

Hide a Jewel

> Choose to love the LORD your God and to obey him and commit yourself to him, for he is your life (Deuteronomy 30:20).

Patience Pays

Read the Clue

Be humble and gentle. Be patient with each other, making allowance for each other's faults because of your love (Ephesians 4:2).

Discover the Treasure

Kerri served customers of all ages at the ice cream shop where she worked during the summer. Three young boys entered the store one hot afternoon. "May I help you?" she asked. The kids peered and pointed through the counter's glass window at two dozen buckets filled with the sweet frozen treat.

"Can I have the bubblegum flavor?" asked one boy.

"Sure," said Kerri. She scooped the blue ice cream and began pressing it into a cone.

"No, wait a minute," said the child. "I changed my mind. I want chocolate marble instead."

"No problem," said Kerri. She removed the bubblegum flavored ice cream and replaced it with chocolate marble. But as she did, the youngster spoke again.

"Stop! I didn't say chocolate marble. I said raspberry ripple."

Kerri hesitated. She took a deep breath and removed the ice cream. "Are you sure you want raspberry ripple?" she asked.

"Yes! Well, maybe not. I want strawberry. Yeah, strawberry for sure."

Kerri held her breath as she scooped the boy's choice and filled a cone. This time he remained silent. He grinned as she handed him the cone. "Thanks!" he said, his eyes twinkling.

The scenario repeated itself when the next child placed his order, and again when the third child asked for his favorite flavor. Kerri completed the last request and smiled at the kids. "Thanks for coming in today," she said. "Enjoy your treats!"

After the boys left the shop, Kerri's boss, Mr. Williams, entered the room. "I overheard what you said to those customers," he said. "Thank you for treating them well. You're obviously a patient person."

Kerri smiled. "I try. Being patient isn't always easy, but it's always worthwhile."

"You're right about that," said Mr. Williams. "I once hired a student who seemed smart and friendly, but before long customers began complaining about his attitude. Apparently, he told children to hurry, and he made nasty comments when they changed their minds. A few parents told me that their kids wanted to come here but were scared to come alone. I spoke with that employee several times and explained that by modeling patience, he could help customers feel welcome and special, but he didn't change. I finally asked him to find a different job. Patience is a valuable quality to possess, and I see it in you."

Just then two girls entered the shop. "May I help you?" asked Kerri.

"I'd like chocolate marshmallow—one scoop, please," said the first girl. Kerri began pressing the ice cream into a cone.

"Wait!" said the girl. "I think I'll have peaches and cream instead. Two scoops."

Kerri glanced at Mr. Williams and grinned. He returned her smile with a wink.

Patience *is* a valuable quality. In fact, God's Word lists it as part of the fruit of the Spirit (Galatians 5:22). What does that mean?

When we become God's children, His Holy Spirit comes to live in us. He changes us from the inside out if we allow Him to. He removes bad qualities, such as impatience, and replaces them with good qualities that show others what God is like. Because God is patient, He wants us to model that virtue too.

What do you do when you feel impatient? Do your actions or words show others what God is like? If not, ask God to change you from the inside out. Ask Him to remove your impatience and give you patience in its place. He'll do it! The process isn't always easy, but it's always worthwhile!

Share the Wealth

Dear God, thank You for being patient with us when we say or do wrong things. Please help us to model patience to others, even when it's difficult to do so. We want Your Holy Spirit to control our lives and produce patience in us (Galatians 5:22). Thank You for hearing our prayer. Amen.

What situations cause you to feel impatient with other people? How can you change?

Hide a Jewel

Encourage those who are timid. Take tender care of those who are weak. Be patient with everyone (1 Thessalonians 5:14).

Motor Mouth

Read the Clue

A truly wise person uses few words (Proverbs 17:27).

Discover the Treasure

Have you ever heard the term *motor mouth?* People use this expression to describe a person who talks nonstop. His tongue wags and his jaw flaps, often with little thought about what he's saying. He simply enjoys talking about this and that and everything else in between.

Jennifer and Jeannie were motor mouths. Twin motor mouths, to be exact. Everywhere they went, they yakked about the weather. They blabbed about their hair. They joked about their neighbors. And they jabbered about their classmates.

Sometimes their nonstop conversation landed them in trouble, as it did when they attended movies. Sitting near the back of the theater, they offered a running commentary about the film.

"What do you think—will the beautiful girl marry the handsome rich guy?" said Jennifer.

"I doubt it. I think she'll marry the cowboy," said Jeannie.

"If she does, she'll have to move to the farm, but she doesn't know how to ride horses or milk cows."

"That's a problem, but hey—she could learn."

"Hey...hay...get it?" The twins giggled at their own joke. Their chatter flew back and forth as they munched their popcorn, slurped their sodas, and smiled at the moviegoers seated in front of them who were scowling and saying, "shhhh!"

The moviegoers weren't the only people who grew annoyed. So did the girls' gymnastics instructor. More than once, their chatter disrupted their concentration and sent them toppling from the balance beam to the floor in a most ungraceful manner. Their school buddies grew frustrated because the twins interrupted them nearly every time they spoke. And in class, the girls' blabbering kept other students from hearing the teacher.

One day their teacher asked the twosome to remain after class. "Young ladies, you talk too much," he said. "You need to learn self-control. Speak when it's appropriate, but otherwise, practice silence."

The twins gawked. *Silence? Self-control?* This was a new concept.

"I have an idea," said the teacher. "I'll buy you each a book if you can do this for one week."

The girls agreed. As they left the room, Jennifer said, "So how difficult do you think this will be?"

"It might be a little tricky," said Jeannie, "but I think we can do it. Starting now!"

For the next seven days, the girls caught themselves whenever they started jabbering for no particular reason. If someone asked them a question, they answered politely. They stopped interrupting and started listening to other people. And they remained silent in class unless talking was appropriate.

To their surprise, no one stared and said "shhhh" at the movie theater. Their gymnastic skills improved. Their classmates enjoyed spending time with them. Their teacher congratulated them for learning well, and he gave them both a new book.

Is the thought of practicing self-control in your speech a new concept, as it was for Jennifer and Jeannie? If so, you're probably not alone. This is a guideline for behavior that we don't often think about.

God's Word says that a wise person uses few words. Perhaps that's because speaking too many words can sometimes cause us to say things we later regret. Sometimes we annoy other people if we talk too much, especially if we prevent them from hearing something they want to hear. Sometimes speaking too many words means we're interrupting other people's conversations, and that's rude behavior. Sometimes speaking too many words leads to complaining or criticizing.

Because God values wisdom, He wants us to be wise. He wants us to behave politely and not to speak words we'll later regret. How can we do this? By speaking few words rather than sounding like a motor mouth.

How difficult do you think this might be? Give it a try, and you'll see!

Share the Wealth

> God, thank You for teaching us how to be wise. Thank You for showing us that being wise means speaking with few words rather than rambling on and on like a motor mouth. Take control of what we say, O Lord, and keep our lips sealed (Psalm 141:3). Amen.

Is interrupting other people a problem in your family? If so, invent a family solution to help the offenders learn to listen more carefully. Think of a kind solution. (No duct tape allowed!)

Hide a Jewel

> Even fools are thought to be wise when they keep silent; when they keep their mouths shut, they seem intelligent (Proverbs 17:28).

Sow and Reap

Read the Clue

Those who live only to satisfy their own sinful desires will harvest the consequences of decay and death. But those who live to please the Spirit will harvest everlasting life from the Spirit (Galatians 6:8).

Discover the Treasure

"Hey, Mom!" Stacy called as she ran into the house after school. "Look at my report card! I aced my math midterm! And my English and social studies grades are higher than I'd expected too!" She flashed a big grin and handed her report card to her mother.

Mom studied the report card and read the teachers' comments: *Stacy uses class time wisely. Her work is always thorough and neat. Her essays are well-written. It's a pleasure to have her in class.*

"Well done," said Mom, smiling. "Your hard work has been worth it." She hugged Stacy and then glanced at the kitchen clock. "By the way, do you know where your brother is? I thought he'd be home by now."

Mom had barely finished her sentence when Stacy's younger brother, Mel, shuffled through the door. He dropped his backpack on the floor, grabbed a granola bar from a basket on the table, and disappeared into the family room without glancing at them or uttering a word. Mom and Stacy watched him in silence and then looked at each other.

"Uh-oh," said Stacy. "Something's wrong."

"You're right about that," said Mom. She poured a glass of milk for her son and followed him into the family room. She found him sulking in front of the television. "Are you okay?" she asked.

"If flunking math can make anyone feel okay, then I guess I'm just fine," said Mel.

"Oh…I understand," said Mom. She offered him the glass of milk. "Your grades weren't what you'd expected. Is that it?"

"That's it. My grades were lousy." Mel accepted the glass and gulped the milk in three swallows. "I'll show you." He retrieved his backpack and handed his report card to his mom. "How could this have happened? I don't understand."

Mom knew. She recalled the evenings when she'd encouraged Mel to study for exams, but he'd busied himself with other activities instead. She recalled his excuses and arguments, and her decision to let him learn a life lesson the hard way. Finally she said quietly, "If you could choose between doing math homework and playing a computer game, which would you select?"

"A computer game."

"And if you could choose between hanging out with your friends and writing an essay, which would you choose?"

"I'd hang out with my friends, of course."

"And if you could choose between good grades and poor grades, which would you prefer?"

"That's a no-brainer. Good grades."

Mom smiled and nodded. "Come with me," she said. She led Mel to the backyard and stopped beside their garden patch. "Do you remember which vegetables we planted last year?"

Mel thought for a moment and answered, "Peas, carrots, beans, cucumbers, and tomatoes, I think."

"Good memory!" said Mom. "Do you remember what vegetables grew?"

"That's an easy question," he said. "Peas, carrots, beans, cucumbers, and tomatoes, of course. That's what we planted, so that's what grew."

"Exactly," said Mom. "We sowed those seeds and we harvested those vegetables. It's impossible to harvest turnips from bean seeds. It's impossible to harvest zucchini if we plant corn. We reap what we sow."

A puzzled expression crossed Mel's face. "I don't get it. What do veggies and grades have in common?"

"You'd be surprised," said Mom. "If you want to harvest good grades, you need to sow the right seeds, like hard work and a good attitude toward your studies. Does that make sense?"

"Yeah," said Mel. He kicked the dirt with his toe. "If I want better grades I'll have to sow more time in the books and less on computer games."

"That's it," said Mom. "Now, let's go inside and take a look at tonight's homework assignment."

Gardeners understand the terms *sowing* and *reaping*. They know that if they want a beautiful display of tulips when spring arrives, they must plant tulip bulbs. Nothing else will do. Mel also understands. He knows that he must sow good study habits if he wants to reap good grades.

But sowing and reaping applies to more than gardens and grades. For example, sowing a friendly attitude toward newcomers at school reaps friendship. Sowing helpfulness at home reaps a happy heart. Sowing kind words reaps encouragement for those who hear them. And sowing the seeds of obedience to God's Word reaps life that never ends.

On the other hand, sowing negative seeds such as anger or fighting words causes only trouble (Job 4:8). We reap jealousy, arguments, and God's disappointment.

Because we reap what we sow, let's be sure to sow wisely!

Share the Wealth

Dear God, we praise You because Your laws remain true today. They make us wiser than our enemies and constantly guide us (Psalm 119:91,98). Thank You for teaching us the

importance of sowing good seeds. Please make us faithful
to sow seeds that please You (Galatians 6:8). Amen.

Parents, help your children understand the importance of this prin-
ciple by discussing several examples. Here's a starter question: "What
do we reap if we sow hours of watching violent movies?" (We might
have bad dreams, and we might begin behaving the same way.)

Hide a Jewel

You will always reap what you sow! (Galatians 6:7).

Smiles and Sandwiches

Read the Clue

If you help the poor, you are lending to the LORD—and he
will repay you! (Proverbs 19:17).

Discover the Treasure

Rain pelted the car's windshield as Troy's family entered the pay
parking lot in their city's downtown district. They'd anticipated this
trip to the science museum for a long time, and nothing—not even a
dismal downpour—could dampen their enthusiasm.

"Let's run!" said Dad as he scooped up Troy's little sister. "The
museum's only two blocks away!" Troy and his mom followed close
behind, laughing and dodging puddles as they ran. The foursome
reached the first intersection just as the traffic light turned red.

Troy glanced up and down the sidewalk as they waited for the
light to change. He noticed several blanket-covered forms huddling in
doorways. A grey-whiskered man in a tattered jacket sat cross-legged
on a piece of cardboard. He held a sign with the words *homeless and
hungry.* The man's eyes met Troy's, and he gave a little nod. The light
turned green before Troy could respond.

"C'mon, let's go before we're all soaked!" said Dad.

The day's fun erased thoughts about the man from Troy's mind. But
during the drive home, the man's face reappeared and lingered in his

thoughts. Finally Troy voiced his concern for the man: "Where does he sleep? What does he eat? Do you think he has a family?"

"The city has several shelters for the homeless," explained Dad, "but I doubt they have enough beds for everyone. Folks like this fellow often sleep in a city park or in a doorway or alley. He probably eats a hot meal at the shelter occasionally. As for having a family—that's anyone's guess."

At the next week's youth group meeting, Troy's pastor spoke about God's desire for His children to help the poor. "How can we obey God in this regard?" he asked.

Once again, Troy thought about the man and his cardboard sign. "If they're hungry, we can feed them," he said.

"That's an excellent idea," said the pastor. "That's something practical we can do as a group. How can we make it happen?"

Suggestions flew back and forth for several minutes. Finally the group formed a consensus: They would host a neighborhood car wash and earn funds to buy bread and sandwich ingredients. Then they would make and distribute sandwiches among the homeless in the city's downtown district. And that's what they did—not just once, but once a month. Their excitement encouraged other youth groups to join the action. Adults also began asking if they could participate.

At first the kids felt nervous, but after the second or third trip, they began recognizing faces and remembering names. These men weren't just homeless strangers anymore; they'd become friends whose faces lit up when they saw them. That, and the joy the kids felt in their own hearts, made the effort worthwhile.

Preparing and distributing sandwiches to the homeless *is* a great idea! But we can care for the poor in many other ways. Within our own community, we can buy diapers for a crisis pregnancy center. We can donate new and used toys and clothing to a shelter for abused women and children.

We can also help the poor beyond our community. We can participate in projects such as the Angel Tree and buy Christmas gifts for prisoners' children (visit www.angeltree.org). We can give money to honest organizations that send aid to the needy after major natural disasters such as earthquakes or floods. Or we can sponsor children overseas. Our family sponsors a young boy in India. Our money helps to provide an education for him and a fresh water supply for his village.

God loves people. He wants us to love them too. Let's ask Him to show us how we can help the poor, and then let's do what He says. We will never be able to help *all* the poor, but our efforts make a difference each time we help one person in need.

Share the Wealth

> Dear God, thank You for loving the poor. You help the fallen and those bent beneath their loads (Psalm 145:14). Help us understand how we can help the poor around us. And help us remember that when we do so, we are lending to You, and You will repay us (Proverbs 19:17). Amen.

How can your family help the poor? Make a plan and do it. You will be blessed as you bless others.

Hide a Jewel

> *Those who oppress the poor insult their Maker, but those who help the poor honor him* (Proverbs 14:31).

The Star Servant

Read the Clue

And since I, the Lord and Teacher, have washed your feet, you ought to wash each other's feet. I have given you an example to follow. Do as I have done to you (John 13:14-15).

Discover the Treasure

Jade spent Saturday afternoon running errands downtown. By the time she'd finished, her arms were filled with shopping bags and a half dozen books she'd borrowed from the public library for a research project. Time had passed quickly. When she glanced at her watch, she realized it was later than she'd thought.

I'd better hurry, thought Jade. *The concert starts at seven o'clock, and I still have to get ready.* She'd purchased tickets two months prior for this concert and didn't want to be late. The star was her favorite singer. She owned all her CDs and could hardly wait to see her perform in person.

Jade dashed for the nearest city bus stop. In her haste, however, she tripped on an uneven sidewalk. She let out a startled cry as she hit the concrete. Shopping bags and books flew in every direction.

A moment later, Jade heard a woman's voice: "Are you okay?" The good Samaritan, a young woman with long blonde hair, helped her stand to her feet. The woman gathered the bags' contents as Jade

41

brushed herself off and checked for scrapes. She picked up the books and stuffed them into the bags.

"It looks like you're heading for the bus stop. I'll carry these for you," said the woman.

"That's not necessary," said Jade. "I'm okay. Thank you for your help. I really appreciate it." She smiled at her rescuer. The blonde woman returned her smile and then walked away. Jade watched her go. *She looks familiar,* she thought. *Where have I seen her?*

That evening, Jade and her best friend sat in the front row at the concert. When the star stepped onto the stage, Jade could hardly believe her eyes. "That's her!" she said to her friend.

"Of course, that's her," her friend said, laughing. "She's the reason we're here, remember?"

"No, no! I mean, she's the woman who helped me when I fell on the sidewalk today!"

"Are you sure?"

"Positive. The long blonde hair is a sure giveaway. I thought she looked familiar—that's because I've seen her face on CD covers and posters."

The singer and her band rocked the auditorium for an hour as the audience clapped and cheered. Between songs, the singer spoke about Jesus Christ. "He was the King of heaven, but He became a servant and lived to help others," she said. "He wants us to do the same. We can make a difference in this world by following His example."

Jade listened closely. She recalled the woman extending a hand to help her stand and collecting the strewn books and bags. And she was excited to know that her favorite singer not only talked about Jesus but also lived like Him.

Jesus shows us how to be a servant. On one occasion, He poured water in a basin and washed His disciples' dirty feet (John 13:1-5). No one liked to do that chore—it was assigned to the household servants. But Jesus didn't mind. He simply did the task without complaining. What a great example!

We too can follow His example by serving others. We can perform simple tasks at home such as setting the dinner table, dusting, or folding laundry. We can help the neighbors by pulling weeds from their flowerbeds or mowing their lawn. We can help in our neighborhood by picking up trash or volunteering for various community programs. Regardless of how old or young we are, we can make a difference in this world by following Jesus' example.

Share the Wealth

Dear God, thank You for sending Jesus to show us how to serve others. He was a King, but He made Himself like a slave and appeared in human form. Help us display the same attitude that Christ had (Philippians 2:5-7). Open our eyes to see opportunities to serve others. Amen.

List three ways your family can serve your neighbors. Now make plans to do those things! Enjoy yourselves!

Hide a Jewel

All of you, serve each other in humility, for "God sets himself against the proud, but he shows favor to the humble" (1 Peter 5:5).

Special Party Guests

Read the Clue

For the whole law can be summed up in this one command: "Love your neighbor as yourself" (Galatians 5:14).

Discover the Treasure

"You're so quiet today. Is something bothering you?"

"No. I'm okay," said Sandi. She stared out the passenger window as she and her mom drove home from soccer practice.

"Are you sure?" asked her mom. "I sense something's on your mind. Maybe I can help."

Sandi shook her head at first, but a moment later she spilled her story. "Marina and her friends invited me to eat lunch with them today. While we were eating, they started planning a party. They listed everyone they want to invite. They included the whole class except the two new girls."

"Perhaps they just forgot to add their names," suggested Mom.

"Nope. I asked them," said Sandi. "They rolled their eyes and said they don't want them to come."

"Did they give a reason?"

"Yeah. They said their skin is the wrong color and they don't speak English well enough."

Mom shook her head but said nothing as she slowed the car and pulled into the family's driveway. She turned off the motor and then turned to face Sandi. "How did you respond?"

"I said I didn't agree. I told them I wasn't interested in a party that left people out for those reasons. I want to welcome the girls to our country, not make them feel like aliens." Sandi's eyes filled with tears. "They said they couldn't understand why I'd want to spend time with them. They said, 'Suit yourself. Throw your own party and invite the losers.'"

Mom hugged Sandi. "I'm so proud of you for doing the right thing," she said. "Hey—did you know that people criticized Jesus for spending time with those they considered losers?"

Sandi listened as her mom spoke about the night Jesus attended a dinner party at Levi's house. Because Levi was a tax collector and considered a crook, the religious leaders were shocked that Jesus would spend time with him. To make matters worse in the Pharisees' opinion, the party guests included other tax collectors and notorious sinners (Mark 2:15). The Pharisees considered themselves too good to associate with these men, but Jesus had a much different attitude.

"Jesus spent time with these men because He cared about them," said Mom. "Your situation is similar. You want to spend time with the new girls because you care about them. Despite what Marina and her friends said, you've done what is right. Your attitude pleases God, and He'll honor you for that."

"So what should I do now?" said Sandi.

Mom smiled and winked. "I have an idea. Let's go in the house and plan a welcome party for a couple of special guests. Does that sound like fun?"

Sandi deserves a big round of applause! The new kids' skin is a different color than hers, and they can't speak her language well, but that doesn't matter to her. She values them because God values them. Her attitude shows love for other people, and that pleases Him.

When we spend time with those whom others consider losers, we might receive criticism. If that happens, let's brush off the harsh words and do what we know to be right. Pleasing God is more important than pleasing other people.

No one's a loser in God's eyes. He loves people, and He wants us to share His love with them. Let's honor Him by showing respect and kindness despite what others may say.

Share the Wealth

Dear God, thank You for loving every person on earth. Thank You for sending Jesus to show us how to do the same. Please help us obey Your commands by teaching us to love others as we love ourselves (Galatians 5:14). Amen.

Do you know someone in your school, neighborhood, or church who others might consider a loser? If so, how can you show respect and kindness to him or her?

Hide a Jewel

Love your neighbor as yourself. I am the LORD (Leviticus 19:18).

Fickle or Faithful?

Read the Clue

There are "friends" who destroy each other, but a real friend sticks closer than a brother (Proverbs 18:24).

Discover the Treasure

Her name was Fiona, but most kids at school called her "Fickle Fiona." That name suited her well. Why? Let me explain...

Fickle Fiona enjoyed meeting new people. In fact, on the first day of school each year, she introduced herself to the new kids in her class: "Hi! I'm Fiona. What's your name?" She toured them around the building and showed them their classrooms, the library, the gym, and the cafeteria. She introduced them to other students, and she always made sure they had a lunch buddy.

The problem was, Fiona acted friendly for about two weeks. That's when the novelty wore off, and she dropped them—*ker-splat!* "I've helped you long enough," she'd say, tossing her silky black hair. "You're on your own now." Her behavior did *not* impress the new students. In fact, she hurt many feelings, but she didn't seem to care.

Last year something unexpected happened about two weeks after Fiona pulled her annual stunt. The school day was only half-finished when her stomach began churning and her head started aching.

"I feel lousy," Fiona told her teacher. A half hour later, her mom drove into the school parking lot and took her home. She crawled into bed and huddled under her blankets. And there she stayed for three long and lonely days, fighting a fever and aching bones.

Fiona began feeling a little better on the fourth day. Late in the afternoon, her mother knocked on her bedroom door. "You have a visitor," she said. She stepped aside to allow the guest to enter the room.

Fiona thought she was hallucinating. Her jaw dropped. Her face flushed. She remembered befriending this girl. She also remembered dumping her. "Hayley?" she stammered. "What are you doing here?"

Hayley placed a backpack on the foot of Fiona's bed. "I brought your homework so you can catch up before returning to class. And I...well, I...I just want to be a good friend."

Fiona struggled to find words. "Thank you," she whispered. "But I haven't been a good friend to you."

Hayley nodded. "You're right about that." Then she smiled and added, "But it's never too late to try again."

Having good friends is important, but *being* a good friend is also important. Fickle Fiona earned her nickname because the friendship she offered was unreliable. It changed according to her whims. Hayley, on the other hand, demonstrated faithfulness. Even though Fiona had treated her unkindly, Hayley showed concern and acted in a loving manner.

God wants us to be faithful, not fickle, friends. Why does He care about this? Because He is faithful and wants us to model His character (Psalm 31:5). If we are His children, He always listens to us, always cares for us, and always walks with us, even though we can't see Him. He loves us all the time, even when we're in a grumpy mood. He never dumps us because He's bored with us and wants to hang out with someone else instead. Isn't that cool?

So how can we model that type of faithful friendship? By being consistent. That means being kind at all times, not just when we feel like it or when others treat us well. Sometimes that requires courage. Sometimes we just have to choose to do what's right even though it's tough.

Being faithful, not fickle, pleases God. And that's the best reason for choosing faithfulness.

Share the Wealth

Dear God, thank You for being a faithful friend (Psalm 31:5). Help us imitate You by being loyal and sticking closer than a brother at all times (Proverbs 17:17; 18:24). Amen.

Read Ruth 1:14-18. How did Ruth demonstrate faithful friendship? What did she give up in order to stay with Naomi?

Hide a Jewel

A friend is always loyal, and a brother is born to help in time of need (Proverbs 17:17).

Promise Keeper

Without wavering, let us hold tightly to the hope we say we have, for God can be trusted to keep his promise (Hebrews 10:23).

Discover the Treasure

Michelle and Eric followed their parents into the church fellowship hall. "Looks like this will be a fun party," Eric whispered to his sister. Streamers and balloons decorated the room. A large hanging banner shouted out, "Congratulations!" Under the banner, a pretty table held a fancy three-tier cake, a glass punch bowl, and snacks of every description.

Aunt and uncles, cousins, and friends greeted them. "Grandma and Grandpa will be so surprised!" said one cousin. "They don't suspect a thing."

The party guests mingled and chatted for about 20 minutes. Suddenly another cousin burst through the hall's back door. "Get ready—they're coming!" Everyone turned and faced the main entrance. A few moments later, the door opened and a grey-haired couple hobbled into the room.

"Surprise!" the crowd shouted.

Grandma slapped her hand over her mouth. Her eyes grew large. "Oh my goodness!" she cried. "What's this all about?"

"We want to celebrate your fiftieth wedding anniversary!" said Eric's dad. "After all, this is a major accomplishment. You deserve a party." He gently took Grandma's arm and guided her to a chair under the hanging banner. Grandpa shuffled behind.

For the next half hour, family and friends presented songs and skits that highlighted special events in the grandparents' marriage. The memories drew laughter and tears. Finally Eric's dad rose.

"I'd like to thank my parents for showing me what it means to be faithful," he said. "The past 50 years have not always been easy but you've loved each other through good times and bad. Dad, when Mom broke her hip, you stayed by her side and nursed her back to health. Mom, when Dad felt discouraged because he didn't have enough work to provide as much for his family as he thought he should, you stood by him and encouraged him not to give up.

"Fifty years ago you made a vow to one other. You promised to love each other no matter what, and you've kept your promise. You've been faithful to your word. Congratulations! You've set a fine example for everyone who knows you."

The crowd burst into applause. Grandpa leaned over and kissed Grandma on the cheek. She blushed and laughed. "Come with me, my bride," he said, offering her his hand. She took it, and they made their way to the anniversary cake. Together they posed for pictures before cutting it and sharing it with their guests.

Several hours later, Eric and Michelle climbed into the family car and headed home with their parents. "That *was* a fun party," said Eric. "Balloons, streamers, cake, cake, and more cake." He rubbed his tummy and grinned at Michelle. "But the best part was when Grandpa kissed Grandma."

"Yes, today was a special day," said Eric's dad, "and Grandma and Grandpa's faithfulness to each other made it possible."

Faithfulness is an admirable quality. Being faithful means we keep our promises the way Grandma and Grandpa kept their promise to love each other no matter what. When we're true to our word, other people know we're trustworthy. They know they can depend on us because we won't suddenly change our minds.

It's hugely important to be faithful when we're married. But faithfulness is a quality we can model long before we get married. For instance, promising to babysit a younger brother or sister and then doing it even though friends invite you to hang out with them at the same time is being faithful. Promising to clean our room and then doing it is being faithful. Promising to do our homework before watching TV and then doing it is modeling faithfulness.

God values faithfulness in us because He is faithful. I'm so glad He is! Can you imagine what life would be like if He said, "I promise to be with you always" and then changed His mind? How would we feel if He promised to answer our prayers but decided not to keep His word? We'd be in big trouble!

Let's remember that God is faithful. And let's ask Him to help us be faithful too.

Share the Wealth

Dear God, we praise You because Your Word holds true, and everything You do is worthy of our trust (Psalm 33:4). Thank You for being faithful to us. Please teach us to follow Your example and be faithful to others. Amen.

Name three people you know who demonstrate faithfulness in their words and actions.

Hide a Jewel

I have chosen to be faithful; I have determined to live by your laws (Psalm 119:30).

Hear and Do

Read the Clue

But if you keep looking steadily into God's perfect law—the law that sets you free—and if you do what it says and don't forget what you heard, then God will bless you for doing it (James 1:25).

Discover the Treasure

Friday morning, 12-year-old Miranda and her 14-year-old brother, Bryce, were gathering their books and backpacks when their mom called for their attention.

"Hey, kids—this is a long weekend, so there's no school on Monday. The weatherman predicts sunshine. Sounds like the perfect setup for a camping trip. What do you say?"

Miranda and Bryce stopped scurrying and stared at her. Their parents had divorced nearly a year ago. Since then, their mom had buried herself in books and busyness, making excuses whenever they wanted to do something fun. Her suggestion delighted them.

"Yeah—that sounds like a great idea!" said Bryce.

"I think so too," said Miranda.

The threesome discussed plans enroute to school. "I'll be home at five o'clock. I'll need your help packing so we can leave town immediately after that," said Mom. "Bryce, you're responsible for the big stuff—tent, sleeping bags, cook stove, and lantern. Be sure to bring two fuel canisters. Miranda, I'll write a menu during my lunch break and e-mail it to the computer at home. You'll be responsible for packing the food. Will you do that?"

Both kids nodded. "Yeah, we'll get the job done," said Bryce. A moment later they leaped from the car and headed into the school.

When classes dismissed later that afternoon, Miranda went straight home, but Bryce didn't. Instead, he played baseball with his buddies. *After all,* he reasoned, *it's only three-thirty. Mom won't be home until five o'clock. I have lots of time to hang out with my friends before doing my work.*

Unfortunately, Bryce lost track of time. When he glanced at his watch, it was a quarter past five. "Gotta go!" he called to his friends.

Mom's car was in the driveway when he arrived at home. "Sorry, Mom," he called as he tossed his backpack into the porch. "I'll have everything ready in a few minutes."

Bryce searched the garage and found the tent, the stove, the lantern, and one fuel canister. *Mom told me to bring two canisters, but I can't find the second,* he thought. *And we're already leaving later than we'd planned, thanks to me. One will probably be enough anyway.* He loaded the equipment into the car's trunk and then stuffed a duffel bag with clean clothes. "Ready!" he said.

Two hours later, they'd pitched their tent and were preparing to cook dinner. Mom struck a match and tried lighting the stove. Nothing happened. She tried again. Nothing.

"That's odd," she said. "This fuel canister must be empty. Bryce, would you please bring me the second canister?"

Bryce's face fell. He said nothing.

"You did bring a second canister, didn't you?" she asked. "I didn't know how much fuel this one held, so I thought we'd play it safe and bring an extra, just in case."

"I'm sorry, Mom," said Bryce. "I heard you, and I said I would do it, but I didn't. It's my fault if we can't eat dinner."

Mom raised her eyebrows. She glanced from Bryce to Miranda, and then her gaze fell on the box of macaroni and cheese she'd opened. "Well, that changes our menu, doesn't it?" she said.

What do you suppose the family ate that night? Raw macaroni noodles? We don't know for sure. But we know *this* for sure: Bryce heard his mom's instructions, but he didn't follow them. As a result, their dinner plans didn't happen as they'd hoped.

In real life, changing our dinner plans isn't a big deal. But hearing instructions and doing them is a big deal because God says so. He tells us to be not only hearers but doers also.

When our parents ask us to do a chore, we need to do it. When our school teachers give us directions for homework, we need to follow them. When God's Word gives us instructions, we're to pay attention and do what they say. God says we're wise when we follow instruction (Matthew 7:24).

So be wise. When you hear instruction, don't forget or ignore it. Just do it, and God will bless you.

Share the Wealth

Dear God, thank You for showing us the importance of hearing and following instructions. Help us listen to Your teaching and obey You, for then we will be wise, like a person who builds a house on a solid rock (Matthew 7:24). Amen.

List three instructions from everyday life that are important to follow. What might happen if we forget or ignore them? Here's a suggestion: Road rules tell drivers to stop at red lights. What happens if drivers don't heed that instruction? Now list three instructions from God's Word. Why is it important to follow those directions?

Hide a Jewel

You know these things—now do them! That is the path of blessing (John 13:17).

Just an Excuse?

Read the Clue

Don't lie to each other, for you have stripped off your old evil nature and all its wicked deeds (Colossians 3:9).

Discover the Treasure

Simon was in the garage filling his bike tires with air when he heard his dad's voice. "Son—there's a phone call for you!" He wiped his hands on his jeans as he entered the family room and then took the phone from his father.

"Hello," said Simon. He listened to the caller and a little frown crossed his face. "It sounds like fun, but I can't do it," he said. "I have to mow the lawn and clean the garage tomorrow. Sorry. Maybe I can help next time." The conversation ended, and Simon hung up.

"What was that about?" asked Dad.

"Casey asked me to help with a car wash tomorrow. It's a fundraiser for his baseball team. I told him I couldn't because I have to do chores."

"You're planning to mow the lawn and clean the garage?" Dad looked puzzled. "Either you're becoming a very responsible and self-motivated young man, or I'm losing my memory. I don't recall asking you to do those things."

Simon laughed. "Don't worry—your brain cells are still working.

You didn't ask me. And don't think I'm *really* going to do those chores. I was just using them as an excuse. I have other plans." He turned to leave the room, but his dad's voice stopped him.

"Wait a minute. I need an explanation," said his father. "You told Casey you'll be mowing the lawn and cleaning the garage, but you have no intention of doing so? Why did you say that?"

Simon shrugged. "Because some other guys asked me to go mountain biking tomorrow, but I couldn't tell Casey about those plans because he wasn't invited. Chores sounded like a good excuse to me."

Dad shook his head. "Son—think about what you've done. You spoke words that were untrue. That's called lying."

"Yeah, so what? That's no big deal. Casey will never know the difference." Simon turned and headed for the garage. "I need to finish fixing my bike for tomorrow's ride."

"Whoa—wait another minute. It *is* a big deal," said Dad. "Lying is sin, and sin is a big deal no matter what. It cost Jesus His life. Besides, because God values truth, He will never lie. As His children, we're to imitate Him.

"Sit down, Simon. We have some serious talking to do."

Simon is fortunate that his dad understands God's mind regarding truthfulness. Many people don't. They speak false words and call them "a fib," or "an excuse," or "a little white lie." They don't understand, or they refuse to believe, that God says false words are lies, and lying is sin.

Because God is perfect, He cannot lie. He always keeps His promises. The Bible says He is faithful in all He says (Psalm 145:13). And because He is, we know that we can trust Him. God wants us to speak the truth so other people know they can trust us too.

If you've ever told a lie, remember that God forgives us when we sin. The Bible says, "But if we confess our sins to him, he is faithful and just to forgive us and to cleanse us from every wrong" (1 John 1:9). If you've lied in the past, take this opportunity to tell God about it. He'll forgive, just as He promised, and He'll help you speak the truth from now on.

Share the Wealth

Dear God, we praise You because all Your words are faithful (Psalm 145:13). Thank You for being truthful. Thank You that You cannot lie, and because of that, we can always trust Your words. Please make us more like You, and help us always speak the truth. Amen.

We suffer consequences when we lie. What are those consequences? What are the benefits for always speaking the truth?

Hide a Jewel

Those who are godly hate lies; the wicked come to shame and disgrace (Proverbs 13:5).

Take Out the Garbage

Read the Clue

So get rid of all the filth and evil in your lives, and humbly accept the message God has planted in your hearts, for it is strong enough to save your souls (James 1:21).

Discover the Treasure

"Michael, please tidy your room and take out the garbage after you finish packing for camp," said Mom.

"Yeah, I will," said Michael.

"Don't forget," said Mom. "This is the third time I've asked you to do those chores."

"I know, I know." Michael finished eating his grilled cheese sandwich and guzzled a glass of milk. Less than 20 minutes remained before he'd leave for a two-week session of summer camp. He could hardly wait. He'd saved his allowance and paper route money for nearly a year. This was going to be the best camp ever!

Michael dashed back to his room. He whistled as he shoved his pillow, a pair of jeans, a couple T-shirts, and a jacket into his duffel bag. He pulled its zipper. "Done!" He took a final glance around his room to ensure that he hadn't forgotten anything important before stepping into the hallway and closing the door behind him. His ride arrived minutes later, and he was gone, headed for the outdoor adventure of a lifetime.

There was only one little problem. Do you know what it was?

Michael remembered to pack all his necessary belongings, but he forgot to tidy his room and take out the garbage. An apple core lay buried beneath his blanket. Two or three others were strewn in strange places, having landed wherever he tossed them several days prior. A brown banana peel sprawled in a corner. A half-empty carton of chocolate milk sat on the windowsill. A leftover tuna sandwich littered his desk. For 14 days, the summer sun shone through Michael's window and warmed his room.

Two weeks later, Michael returned home. He lugged his duffel bag to his bedroom and threw open the door. Curious odors smacked him in the face. "Gross!" he exclaimed. "What's that smell? M-o-m!"

Michael's mom was watering plants on the deck when she heard his voice. "What's wrong, son?" she asked.

"My room stinks," he whined.

"No kidding," she said. "And why, do you think, does it stink?"

Michael shrugged. "I don't know. It just does."

"Look around your room. Think again."

Michael glanced around the room and groaned. "Oh yeah...I was supposed to clean up before I left for camp, but I didn't."

Michael could have sulked about the terrible smell, but thankfully, he opened his window instead. He tossed one item after another into his garbage can. And then he did what his mom asked him to do two weeks prior—he took the garbage out. His work paid off. Before long, his room was tidy, and the bad smell was gone.

Did you know that sin is like garbage? That's right! If we allow sin to live in us the way Michael allowed garbage to stay in his room, things eventually turn ugly.

God knows that, so He says, "Get rid of all the filth and evil in your lives, and humbly accept the message God has planted in your hearts." What filth is He talking about? Not apple cores and banana peels. He's referring to behavior such as lying, cheating, thinking bad thoughts, disobeying our parents, treating others unkindly, being lazy, being jealous of others, and more. Those things are called *sin*, and God thinks sin is gross.

He wants us to get rid of the filth so His message can live in our hearts. What's that message? It's the story of His love for us. You see, God says our sin deserves a punishment. But He loves us so much that He sent His sinless Son, Jesus, to take our punishment when He died on the cross. When we believe He died for us and He rose from the dead three days later, we are saved. That means we can live forever in heaven with Him someday.

Sin, like garbage, is gross, but living in heaven with God forever— that's great!

Share the Wealth

> Dear God, thank You for loving us so much that You made it possible for us to get rid of the garbage in our lives. Thank You that Your message is strong enough to save our souls (James 1:21). Please help us live clean lives to honor You. Amen.

What sinful garbage is hiding in your life? Tell God about it and ask Him to clean your heart.

Hide a Jewel

> *Get rid of all bitterness, rage, anger, harsh words, and slander, as well as all types of malicious behavior. Instead, be kind to each other, tenderhearted, forgiving one another, just as God through Christ has forgiven you* (Ephesians 4:31-32).

Stamp Out Jealousy

Read the Clue

Let us not become conceited, or irritate one another, or be
jealous of one another (Galatians 5:26).

Discover the Treasure

"I can hardly wait for tomorrow," Randy said as he dribbled a basketball past his buddies Chris and Pete. He shot the ball toward the
basket. It rolled once around the rim before falling through the hoop.
"Yes!" he said. "Two points!"

The boys had played basketball after school every day for a month
to prepare for team tryouts. They'd improved their skills and played
well during the tryouts, and they felt confident that they'd be selected.
Tomorrow they'd know for sure because the coach had promised to
post the players' names.

The next morning, Randy met Chris and Pete at the school gym.
They waited together until the coach arrived and pinned the list of
names to a bulletin board. The boys eagerly scanned the list. Of their
three names, only Pete's appeared.

"I'm in!" said Pete. "Wahoo! I guess my practice paid off!" He
grinned and slapped his friends' shoulders.

Randy smiled at Pete. "Way to go," he said as he punched his friend's
arm playfully. "You worked hard. You deserve it."

Chris said nothing. He turned and walked away, shaking his head as Randy and Pete began talking about the season's game schedule.

Later that morning, Randy found Chris at his locker between classes. "It's too bad for us, but it's great for Pete, eh?" he said.

"I don't believe it," said Chris.

"What do you mean?"

Chris glared at Randy. "I mean, how was Pete chosen for the team? Everyone knows we're better players than he is. And I can't believe you're so happy for him. What's with you anyway?"

Randy shrugged. "Hey—I know you're disappointed. So am I. But why should I be upset about the coach choosing Pete and not you or me? Pete worked hard. Tryouts were fair. The coach wants to pick a winning team, and if he wants Pete to be part of it, that's his business."

"It's not fair. We'd be good team players too."

Randy paused as he pondered his friend's words. "I'm not sure that's true right now, Chris. Good team players cheer for each other. They're happy when another person does well. They don't let jealousy make them angry."

Chris stared at his feet. "Right now I *do* feel angry. I don't even want to talk with Pete. I don't want to shoot baskets with him anymore. The fun's gone."

"Well, you can change that," said Randy. "Come to my house after school, like always. Pete's coming too. He's nervous about playing the first game this weekend and wants more practice. Let's give him a good challenge. And we can cheer for him at the games. What do you say?"

Chris closed his locker and faced his friend. "I guess so. Maybe you're right. I don't want to be angry at my friends. Besides, I'd miss all the action if I stayed home."

If Chris stayed home because he felt jealous of Pete's success, he'd miss more than just the basketball action. He would also miss Pete's friendship. You see, jealousy separates friends. Rather than feeling happy for another's success, a jealous person feels angry. A person who is angry has a hard time being with other people or feeling happy for them when they do well.

God's Word warns us against being jealous of others. It says that jealousy comes from the devil. And where jealousy lives, other evil will be found (James 3:15-16).

Because God loves us and wants the best for us, He tells us to be gentle and willing to yield to others (James 3:17). When others succeed, we're to encourage them with our words and our actions. We might not always feel like doing that, but when we choose to do what's right, the feelings often follow.

Share the Wealth

> Dear God, thank You for loving us and showing us how to live. Please remove any feelings of jealousy that we have toward others. Help us to be peace loving and gentle. Help us live lives that are full of mercy and good deeds (James 3:17). Amen.

Do you feel jealous toward anyone? Perhaps a friend won an award that you'd hoped to win, or someone has a nicer bike or cuter clothes or a bigger allowance. How can you encourage that person?

Hide a Jewel

> And those who are peacemakers will plant seeds of peace and reap a harvest of goodness (James 3:18).

Strike Out Temper Tantrums

Read the Clue

> Be quick to listen, slow to speak, and slow to get angry. Your anger can never make things right in God's sight (James 1:19-20).

Discover the Treasure

"Batter up!" shouted the ump.

Keith marched to home plate swinging his favorite bat. The other team was ahead by one run. With two runners out in the bottom of the ninth inning and no one on base, his team needed a home run. And he was determined to deliver.

The pitcher rubbed the ball, put on his glove, started his windup, and let 'er rip.

"Steee---rike!"

"Strike? Are you kidding me?" said Keith. "That was way outside the plate."

"No back talk," warned the ump.

The pitcher glared at Keith as he wound up and threw the ball a second time. A split second later it whizzed past him.

"Strike TWO!"

Keith moaned. "What's wrong with your eyes?" he said to the ump. "You need glasses!"

"One more comment like that and you're out of the game," said the ump.

Once again the pitcher wound up. The ball streaked across the plate before Keith saw it coming.

"Strike THREE! You're out!"

"You don't know what you're talking about!" yelled Keith. He heaved the bat. It hit the ground with a thud and bounced on the dirt as he stormed off the field.

"Wait a minute," shouted the ump. "Come back here."

Keith retraced his steps, hands on hips. He looked at the ump and cocked his head. "What? I didn't do anything wrong," he snorted. "Am I in trouble?"

"Yeah, you're in trouble—in more ways than one," said the ump. "First, throwing temper tantrums isn't acceptable here or anywhere else. I'm the ump and I make the calls. You can disagree with me but not by yelling. And heaving the bat is never appropriate behavior. That bat might have hit someone and caused serious damage. Sorry, Bud, but you won't be playing the next game in this tournament."

Keith scowled. "But I..." he began.

"Stop," said the ump. He held up his hand to silence the boy. "Your baseball tantrum landed you in trouble with the game, but you're headed for more serious trouble unless you learn to deal with your anger."

Keith fell silent when he heard the ump's words. He'd heard similar warnings—from his dad and his coach. He'd brushed them off before. But this time, they stuck to his conscience. And this time he decided to listen.

Whew! I'm glad Keith decided to pay attention to the wise warning. His angry outburst deserved the ump's discipline. If he continued throwing tantrums in other parts of his life, he would likely fall into major trouble someday.

Today's clue warns us about anger: "Your anger can never make things right in God's sight." In fact, anger usually makes things all wrong. For instance, what happens if you explode at a younger sibling who enters your room uninvited? What happens if you throw a fit when your folks tell you to do something you don't feel like doing? I promise you one thing—whatever happens, it isn't pretty.

Feeling angry isn't wrong, but if we let it control us and our behavior, it often leads to sin. The Bible says that it gives a foothold to the devil (Ephesians 4:27). God doesn't want His children to suffer the consequences of sin, so He warns us to control our temper. "Be slow to anger," He says (James 1:19).

When you feel angry about something, send God a quick prayer. Say, "God, help! Show me what to do, and keep me from doing something wrong!" He might tell you to walk away from the situation. He might tell you to sit down and cool off for a while. If an idea comes to your mind that will help you not lose your temper, do it. You'll be glad you did.

Share the Wealth

> Dear God, thank You that You can help us control our temper. Please make us quick to listen, slow to speak, and slow to get angry (James 1:19). Amen.

When your family members feel angry, how do they act? Talk about ways to handle anger. For example, leaving the room for a few minutes often helps an angry person cool down. It also helps to talk about the reasons for feeling angry. "I feel angry because..."

Hide a Jewel

> *Don't sin by letting anger gain control over you* (Ephesians 4:26).

Hiding!

Read the Clue

You may be sure that your sin will find you out (Numbers 32:23).

Discover the Treasure

Have you ever tried to hide something you'd done because you were afraid of getting into trouble for it? I have. I recall two specific incidents that happened a long, long time ago. The first took place when I was about six years old.

One of my favorite snacks was raspberry-flavored Jell-O powder—dry. I didn't want my mom to know because I thought she'd stop me from eating it. So one afternoon when she was outside, I dragged a chair across the floor and shoved it against the kitchen cabinet. I climbed onto the chair, grabbed a box from the shelf, and stuffed it into a pocket. The deed done, I quickly returned the chair to its place at the table. I'd committed the perfect crime. No one would ever know. Or so I thought.

Mom mowed the lawn a few days later. When she finished, she entered the house wearing a puzzled expression. In her hands she held a half-empty box of raspberry-flavored Jell-O powder. "This is the strangest thing I've ever seen," she said. "Imagine—a Jell-O tree. Do you know anything about this, Grace?"

I could not tell a lie. The lawn, not much larger than a postage stamp, held two small evergreen trees. Afraid to bring my sneaky snack into the house lest my crime be discovered, I'd stuffed it between the boughs of one of those trees. And wouldn't you know it—Mom spied it while mowing the lawn. Thankfully she dismissed the offense with a mere lecture about asking before taking things from the cupboard.

You might think I'd learned my lesson about hiding my wrong-doings. Not so. When I was 14 years old, I tried it again. This time, however, I hid something much riskier than Jell-O powder.

Several friends and I had started experimenting with cigarettes. We bought a package and rode our bikes to a nearby park where we lit up behind some bushes. We coughed and gagged on the smoke while pretending to be professional puffers. Then we popped chewing gum in our mouths lest anyone smell our charcoal breath and discover our dastardly deed.

There was a problem: We couldn't store our cigarettes in the bushes because rain might soak our secret stash, so my friends elected me to find a suitable hiding place. I took the package home and stuffed it between my bed's mattress and box spring. Trouble was, I shared my bedroom with my older sister, who happened to have a phenomenal sense of smell.

A day or two later, my sister and her best friend confronted me. "We know what you've hidden in your bed," they hissed. "Get rid of those smokes or we're telling. When Mom and Dad find out, you'll be toast."

These were no idle threats. I knew I was in big trouble. I tossed the cigarettes and never bought another pack.

Kids aren't the only ones who try to hide stuff they shouldn't be doing. Adults do it too. I know—I've done it. Perhaps your parents have as well. But I've finally figured out that hiding sin takes more effort than it's worth. Besides, it displeases God. And that's reason enough to stop doing it.

Now *you* know my secrets, but guess what—God knew them all along. His Word tells us that we can try to cover our sins, but it's impossible. He sees all the things we do, and He has amazing ways of helping others see them too.

Rather than trying to hide our wrongdoings, we should stop doing those things that displease God. We should tell Him what we've done and ask for forgiveness. Then we don't have to worry about being caught and punished. We can enjoy each day to the full, and that's the best way to live!

Share the Wealth

> Dear God, Your Word says to turn from godless living and to be devoted to You. Please help us do that. Help us remember that Jesus died to set us free from all evil and to make us totally committed to doing what is right. Please teach us to practice self-control and right conduct (Titus 2:12-14). Amen.

Read Genesis 3:1-8. What did Adam and Eve do after they disobeyed God's command not to eat from a certain tree? Did they succeed? Rather than making excuses for their sin, what should they have done? What should we do rather than trying to hide our wrongdoing?

Hide a Jewel

If we confess our sins to him, he is faithful and just to forgive us and to cleanse us from every wrong (1 John 1:9).

Giving Good Gifts

Read the Clue

For God so loved the world that he gave his only Son, so that everyone who believes in him will not perish but have eternal life (John 3:16).

Discover the Treasure

"All right! This is exactly what I wanted!" said Gina. She held up a powder blue sweatshirt that sported a well-known name brand and a hood. "Thanks, Mom. This is the best birthday gift ever." She slipped the sweatshirt over her head and disappeared into the bathroom, where she admired it in the mirror. "I can't wait to show my friends," she called down the hall.

Gina's birthday sweatshirt became her favorite piece of clothing. She especially loved the feel of its fuzzy fleece lining. She liked that its color suited her blonde hair and drew compliments from her friends.

One day, about a month after her birthday, Gina heard terrible news: Hurricane Katrina had devastated the city of New Orleans. Flood waters left countless people straddling rooftops or stranded in attics. Thousands sought safety in a sports complex while many more huddled on freeways. Rescuers worked day and night to save the storm's survivors.

The flood forced many of the city's residents to flee to other cities and states. They arrived wearing the only clothes they had left. Several families moved to Gina's town.

The community immediately offered support for the newcomers. People gave them used cars. Local businesses offered work. Grocery stores supplied food. And a newspaper article asked for donations—furniture, dishes, towels, bedding, and clothing.

Gina read the article and wondered how she could help. Then an idea popped into her mind: *Give your blue sweatshirt to a girl who needs it.*

No way! Gina thought.

Yes. Give the sweatshirt to a girl who needs it more than you do.

A mental argument followed.

But it was my favorite birthday gift.

So what?

But Mom gave it to me. Maybe she won't want me to give it away.

Ask her.

Gina's conscience wouldn't let her sleep that night. Her imagination wandered to the scenes she'd seen on television—frightened people on rooftops waving at rescue boats and helicopters. When morning dawned, she carried her sweatshirt to the kitchen where her mom was preparing breakfast.

"Mom, I have a question."

"Sure, what is it, Gina?"

"Would you be angry with me if I gave this sweatshirt away?"

Gina's mom stopped and stared. "Why would you do that? Don't you like it anymore?"

"I love it. That's the problem."

"I'm puzzled," said her mom. "Help me understand what you're thinking."

"It's like this." Gina proceeded to explain the still, small voice that was urging her to give the sweatshirt to a flood victim, a girl who needed it more than she did. "But I like it so much, Mom. I don't really want to give it away, but these people need help. I think it's the right thing to do."

Mom smiled and hugged Gina. "It sounds as though God is speaking to you," she said. "He loves to give good gifts to people. And that sweatshirt would be an ideal gift for a girl your size. Go ahead—give it away. God will bless you for obeying His voice."

Do you think Gina did the right thing? Do you think it was easy for her? If you answered yes to the first question and no to the second, you're right. She sensed God telling her to give the shirt away, but obeying wasn't easy. After all, the sweatshirt had been a birthday gift from her mother. It fit just right. And it looked great on her. Nevertheless, she cared about the flood victims, so she washed it, wrapped it, and presented it to a very appreciative girl her age.

Giving is something we do when we love as God does. The Bible says that God loved the people in the world so much that He *gave* His Son to take their punishment for sin. Giving His Son must have hurt Him a lot. Nevertheless, He did it because He loved us.

How can you show love to others by giving?

Share the Wealth

> Dear God, thank You for loving us so much that You sent Your Son to die for us (John 3:16). Help us give freely to others so they might feel Your love flowing through us. Amen.

Acts 20:35 says, "You should remember the words of the Lord Jesus: 'It is more blessed to give than to receive.'" Maybe you've given a good gift to someone in the past. If so, how did God bless you for doing so? If you haven't yet given a good gift to someone in need, what can you do in the future?

Hide a Jewel

> *Whatever is good and perfect comes to us from God above, who created all heaven's lights* (James 1:17).

Be a Do-Gooder

Read the Clue

Don't get tired of doing what is good. Don't get discouraged and give up, for we will reap a harvest of blessing at the appropriate time. Whenever we have the opportunity, we should do good to everyone, especially to our Christian brothers and sisters (Galatians 6:9-10).

Discover the Treasure

Kelli watched as Aunt Peggy bagged homemade chocolate chip cookies. She placed a dozen treats in each package, attached a sparkly red bow, and placed the goodies in a wicker basket.

"You're drooling, Kelli," teased Aunt Peggy. "Here—eat a cookie. Maybe it will fix your problem before you drench my kitchen counter." She laughed.

"Yuck! That's gross!" said Kelli. She giggled and took the cookie from Aunt Peggy. "Thanks. Now watch this." The cookie vanished in two bites. "Are you impressed?"

"You betcha. Swallowing a cookie in two bites takes a lot of talent." The duo shared another laugh.

Kelli enjoyed spending time with her favorite aunt. She was young, single, and seemed to be enthusiastic about everything. Best of all, she loved performing random acts of kindness for other people, and she often invited Kelli's participation. The two had spent that Saturday afternoon baking because she wanted to surprise her coworkers with the treats on Monday morning.

The task complete, the twosome popped in a CD, plopped onto the couch, and planted their feet on a stool. "So what's next?" said Kelli.

"That's all I had planned for today," said Aunt Peggy, "but keep next Saturday open on your calendar. I'm inviting my Sunday school class for games and pizza. Perhaps we'll go swimming in the afternoon too."

"Sounds like fun," said Kelli. She thought of her aunt's class—a dozen lucky fourth grade girls. "I'll help chop onions and peppers, and I'll grate the cheese." She paused for a moment and then said, "May I ask you a question?"

"Sure."

"Do you ever get tired of doing nice things for other people?" Kelli paused and bit into another cookie before she continued. "I mean, nearly every weekend you do something kind for someone else. What about yourself? You could go shopping, or hang out with friends all day in your favorite coffee shop, or do whatever you want."

Aunt Peggy pondered her answer before replying. "No, I don't get tired of doing nice things for other people. Don't worry about me—I have lots of time for myself. The way I see it, I want to live life to the fullest, and that means making a difference in other people's lives. Bringing a smile to their faces makes me feel good inside. But that's not my main reason for doing kind things."

That piqued Kelli's curiosity. "What's your main reason?"

"I do what I do because God's Word commands it. He says we're to do good things to everyone whenever we have the opportunity. Believe me, there are more opportunities than I can possibly imagine. Sometimes they involve doing kind things for people who don't really care or even bother to say thanks. But that's okay. I just do what I can, and I know God will bless me. In fact, He already has—He's given me the world's most fantastic niece!"

Kelli grinned. "I think you're great. So do the girls in your Sunday school class. And by the way, when I help with the pizza party next Saturday, is it okay if I teach them to swallow a cookie in two bites?"

As a follower of Jesus Christ, Aunt Peggy wants her life to please Him. She understands that He wants His children to make a difference in the world. As a result, she looks for opportunities to show His love to other people. She does this in simple ways, and people understand the language of love. They know she cares about them. When she tells them about Jesus, they listen.

Regardless of your age, you too can make a difference by doing good things. Think of people around you—teachers, classmates, parents, brothers and sisters, other relatives, neighbors, pastors. Think of one thoughtful deed you can perform on their behalf and then do it. Then think of another kind deed for another person and do it too. Keep it going!

Remember—do good to everyone whenever you have the opportunity, and don't grow weary, especially when they forget to say thanks. God promises a harvest of blessing.

Share the Wealth

> Dear Father, thank You for teaching us to do good for other people. Please make us aware of opportunities and help us not grow weary or discouraged. Thank You for promising to bless us in due time (Galatians 6:9-10). Amen.

How can your family show ongoing kindness to an individual or family? You don't have to spend a lot of money or take a lot of time. Here's one suggestion to kick-start your thinking: Adopt a senior on your street. Give homemade treats if that's appropriate for his or her diet, make homemade cards, rake leaves, and assist with grocery shopping.

Hide a Jewel

> *Dear brothers and sisters, never get tired of doing good* (2 Thessalonians 3:13).

Whoppers and Forgiveness

Read the Clue

You must make allowance for each other's faults and forgive the person who offends you. Remember, the Lord forgave you, so you must forgive others (Colossians 3:13).

Discover the Treasure

Laura ran into her room and slammed the door behind her. She threw herself across her bed. "I can't believe Ellie would do such a thing!" she sobbed into her pillow.

The commotion startled her older sister, Tamara, who was doing homework at her desk across the room. "Are you okay?" she asked.

"No!" came Laura's muffled reply.

Tamara slipped across the room and knelt beside Laura's bed. "I don't know what happened today, but it obviously wasn't nice. Do you want to talk about it?"

Laura rolled onto her side and began spilling her story between sobs. "Ellie and I...were partners...on a social studies report. The teacher told us...to split up the work...I read lots of books...and wrote the whole report. Ellie drew a map and colored it...She brought it to school on the day the report was due...It was so sloppy—I asked her if she could fix it quickly. But she said no...she said she thought it was fine." Laura stopped talking and wiped her tears.

"And then what happened?" asked Tamara.

Laura drew a deep breath and continued. "The teacher gave us our grades today…We got an A on the report and a D on the map. Our map got the lowest grade in the class…When Ellie found out, she told the whole class that I'd drawn the map and she'd written the report. I said that wasn't true…but she called me a liar. No one talked to me for the rest of the day. They all treated me like a criminal. I can't believe she would do such a mean thing—I've never done anything mean to her!" Laura hid her face in her pillow again.

Tamara rubbed her sister's back. "I'm sorry she hurt you," she said. She waited a few seconds and then said quietly, "What do you plan to do about it?"

"I don't know. Maybe I'll tell a whopper about her. I'll spread a story that will make her look like a rotten person. Then no one will want to be her friend."

No one spoke for a minute as Tamara pondered her sister's words. Finally she said softly, "You might want to rethink your idea."

"No way!" Laura pounded her fist on the bed. "You're not helping me! You don't understand!"

"Oh yes I do. Do you remember when someone at school snitched my research notes for a big project last year?" Laura nodded but her face remained buried in her pillow. "I had to repeat my research, so my paper was late for the deadline and my grade was automatically lowered. That person scored a higher grade than me. I felt really angry and wanted to make her pay for what she'd done. But something stopped me."

Laura lifted the pillow from her head, rolled onto her side again, and looked at Tamara. "What happened?"

"Mom reminded me that because God forgives us when we do wrong things, He expects us to do the same for others. In fact, He says He won't forgive us if we won't forgive those who hurt us."

Laura propped herself on one elbow. "But forgiving Ellie would be like saying that what she did was okay."

"No, it's not," said Tamara, shaking her head. "It's saying that you're choosing to do what's right regardless of what she does. And it's trusting God to show her where she's wrong. Can you do that?"

"I'll think about it," said Laura.

Laura has some major thinking to do, doesn't she? Forgiving those who hurt us is often a difficult task, but God tells us to do it anyway. And when He gives a command, He always gives us the ability to do it.

Why does God want us to forgive others even when they do mean things? Because doing so keeps our minds from thinking nasty thoughts about them. It protects our hearts from anger. It fills us with peace. It puts a smile on our face and helps us treat them kindly. Most important, it shows God's love to them. And understanding His love for them might change their lives.

Share the Wealth

Dear God, thank You for being faithful to forgive our sins when we confess them to You (1 John 1:9). When people hurt us, please help us to forgive them just as You forgive us. Thank You for giving us the ability to do Your commands. Amen.

Matthew 18:21-22 says, "Peter came to him and asked, 'Lord, how often should I forgive someone who sins against me? Seven times?' 'No!' Jesus replied, 'seventy times seven.'" Do the math—how many times does Jesus want us to forgive those who hurt us? Does that mean we can stop forgiving after we've forgiven 490 times? If not, what is Jesus talking about?

Hide a Jewel

If you forgive those who sin against you, your heavenly Father will forgive you. But if you refuse to forgive others, your Father will not forgive your sins (Matthew 6:14-15).

A Real Hero

Read the Clue

If your enemies are hungry, feed them. If they are thirsty, give them something to drink, and they will be ashamed of what they have done to you (Romans 12:20).

Discover the Treasure

Jared and his friends attended the same summer camp for several years. They enjoyed everything about it—canoeing, hiking, sailing, archery, kneeboarding, and of course, eating. They also enjoyed meeting new kids who came from far and near to participate in the camping program.

Last summer, however, was different.

Nine boys and one counselor shared Jared's tent. Eight of those boys were fun loving and good-natured. The ninth—David—was the opposite. When the group hiked through the woods, David shoved his way to the front of the line. He did the same when the boys lined up to take turns kneeboarding. At the archery range, he insisted on shooting arrows before anyone else.

For the first day or two, Jared and his friends thought David was only rude. But then the mean behavior began. Jared was standing at the edge of a wooden raft preparing to dive when David pushed him from behind. Jared's feet slipped and he splashed—smack!—on his belly.

"Ha! That was a lousy dive!" said David. He laughed when Jared's head popped to the water's surface.

"Thanks a lot," said Jared as he began swimming toward the raft. He didn't laugh. He didn't even smile.

"What's wrong, poor sport? Did you forget to take diving lessons when you were a little boy?" said David.

Jared ignored the taunt, and that irritated David. When he tried climbing the ladder onto the raft, David pushed him off. Rather than fight, Jared returned to shore and then spent the rest of the afternoon canoeing.

Later that day, Jared returned to the tent to change into dry clothes. He reached into his backpack for his watch, but he couldn't find it. He searched through his duffel bag, but it wasn't there. Then he saw it lying on the tent floor—its face had been smashed.

What happened? Jared wondered as he examined it. His stepdad had given him the watch for his birthday a month ago. It was his favorite gift.

David stepped into the tent as Jared stared at the broken watch. "What's wrong, big boy? Did something happen to your favorite toy?"

Jared looked at David in disbelief. "Did you do this?" he asked, holding up the watch.

"I wouldn't tell you if I did."

Jared's temper flared. He felt like throwing himself at David, pinning him to the ground for the whole world to see. A split second passed as Jared restrained himself. In that moment, David let out a sharp cry. "Ow! Uh-oh—I'm in trouble! Get help, fast!"

"What's wrong?" asked Jared.

"I think a bee stung me! I'm allergic!"

Jared's sister was allergic to bee stings. He knew the danger David faced. Enemy or not, Jared dropped the watch on his sleeping bag and ran from the tent hollering for the camp nurse.

After fireside that evening, Jared's counselor thanked him for saving David's life. "The other guys told me that David bullied you on the raft," he said. "I also know that David broke your watch—he told me so. You probably felt like bullying him back, but you didn't. Well done, hero!"

"I don't feel like a hero," said Jared. "I just did what I was supposed to."

"Not everyone does," said his counselor. "Many folks strike back when someone does mean things to them. That would have been easy for you to do. Instead, you showed love. Only a real hero would act that way."

Jared *is* a real hero for showing love for his enemy. Doing so isn't easy. When someone does something hurtful, our natural tendency is to defend ourselves or seek revenge. But God's Word tells us to love our enemies and bless those who give us a hard time.

Jesus gave us the perfect example when the soldiers hung Him on a cross to die. The leaders laughed, and the soldiers mocked him (Luke 23:33-37). Because He was God, Jesus could have used His power to get revenge and free Himself, but He didn't. Instead, He prayed for their forgiveness.

When someone treats you unkindly, follow Jesus' example. Rather than returning evil for evil, ask God to give you patience and love for that person. And ask Him to change that person's heart.

Share the Wealth

Dear God, when people treat us unkindly, help us to love them with genuine affection and treat them with honor (Romans 12:10). These attitudes are not easy for us, but You're God, and You're able to do anything. We depend on You to help us behave in ways that please You. Amen.

Imagine there's a bully at school. List three ways you can show love to this person.

Hide a Jewel

Don't let evil get the best of you, but conquer evil by doing good (Romans 12:21).

Others First

Read the Clue

Be humble, thinking of others as better than yourself. Don't think only about your own affairs, but be interested in others too, and what they are doing (Philippians 2:3-4).

Discover the Treasure

Jerry liked school, but he *loved* Fridays. They signaled the start of a weekend—two days to hang out with his friends and do fun stuff. This weekend promised to be extra special because his parents had offered to drive him and a buddy to a nearby ski resort to spend Saturday afternoon snowboarding! The ski hill had opened only one week prior, and the conditions were perfect.

The phone rang on Friday evening as Jerry waxed his snowboard. His mom answered with a cheery hello, but her tone quickly changed. "How can we help?" she asked. Concern etched her face as she listened to the caller's reply. "Don't worry about a thing. We're happy to do everything we can." His mother prayed a short prayer and then hung up.

"What's wrong?" asked Jerry. "You look scared."

"That was our neighbor, Mrs. Baker," said Mom. "She needs a

ride to the hospital. Her husband was involved in a car accident on his way home from work, and it looks as though he'll be there for several days. In the meantime, she needs a babysitter until her sister arrives to help on Sunday, and she needs someone to stack the load of firewood that was delivered earlier this week. I told her we'd be glad to help. "

Jerry stopped waxing and stared. "But Mom, we have plans for tomorrow. Remember? Snowboarding?"

"I know you're disappointed, Jerry, but this family's in crisis," said Mom. "This is an opportunity for us to show Christ's love to them by putting their needs ahead of our own needs or wants. Now, I'll drive Mrs. Baker to the hospital. Would you mind watching the kids until I return in an hour or so?"

Jerry felt like saying, "No, thanks. Babysitting isn't exactly my idea of a good time," but he knew it wasn't worth the effort. His mom was already walking toward the front door, car keys in hand.

Moments later, they pulled into the Bakers' driveway. Mrs. Baker's eyes looked red and puffy when she opened the door. She pointed at a piece of paper on the table. "There's the hospital's phone number in case you need me," she said. She kissed her two little boys goodnight and then dashed toward the car. Halfway there, she turned around and called, "Thank you, Jerry. I appreciate this more than you can imagine."

"Yeah, whatever," Jerry muttered as he closed the door. The pre-schoolers stared at him, wearing bewildered expressions. Their bottom lips quivered.

Compassion suddenly filled Jerry's heart. *Poor kids,* he thought. *They don't understand what's happening. I've gotta do something for them.*

"Hey, guys, come here," he said. "Let's read a book. Bring me your favorites." The preschoolers sat on either side of him as he read. Gradually they relaxed and cuddled closer to him. Fifteen minutes later, he finished reading the last story. "Do you like piggyback rides?" he asked. Next came hide-and-seek. Then the trio blew and popped soap bubbles. Jerry was just about to put on a video for the boys when his mom arrived.

"Thank you, Jerry," Mom said. "I'm so glad we were available to Mrs. Baker. I've spoken to her about Christ's love in the past, but helping her in a crisis is a hands-on way to show her what His love looks like. What do you say—shall we give up this weekend for her family's sake and make another date for snowboarding?"

Jerry nodded. "Let's do that. You know something? Babysitting was actually fun. I'll help you watch the kids tomorrow too." And with that, he hoisted the boys on his knees and bounced them until they burst into giggles.

Jerry demonstrated humility by setting his plans aside to help the Baker family. And what happened? He experienced the joy that comes when we do what pleases God.

God's Word says that demonstrating humility is important. We're to care not only about our own well-being but also about the needs of others. When we put their needs before our own, we're showing the same attitude that Christ had when He died for us on the cross.

Your family can experience joy by modeling the behavior that God values. Here are three suggestions:

- Participate in the Angel Tree project at Christmas. This encourages prisoners' children. (See www.angeltree.org.)

- Sponsor a less fortunate child year-round through programs such as World Vision or Compassion International.

- For a month, save the money you might have spent on frills such as eating in a restaurant, renting videos, and buying junk food. Donate that amount to a local charity such as the Salvation Army or a shelter for battered women and children.

Share the Wealth

Dear God, thank You for modeling humility through Jesus, who put our needs ahead of His own desires when He died on the cross for us. Thank You for rewarding Him for His actions (Philippians 2:7-9). We love You! Amen.

Putting other people's needs ahead of our own desires shows humility. How did Jerry practice humility? How can your family model humility toward each other?

Hide a Jewel

The LORD mocks at mockers, but he shows favor to the humble (Proverbs 3:34).

Duck Do's and Don'ts

Read the Clue

The path of the upright leads away from evil; whoever follows that path is safe (Proverbs 16:17).

Discover the Treasure

Two fluffy yellow balls peeped and chirped as my husband, Gene, lifted them from a cardboard box and set them on the floor. "Hey kids," he called. "Mom and I have a surprise for you!"

Our kids had begged for another pet. They already owned Frosty the hamster and Scooter the Russian tortoise, but they wanted another. Gene had suggested ducks. When he was a boy, a friend had given him two ducks as a birthday gift. At first he thought that was a silly present for a boy his age, but he'd soon grown to enjoy the birds. "You might enjoy them too," he'd said. The kids agreed.

Ducks seemed like a logical pet choice for another reason: We lived on a lakeshore. They could swim in our front yard. Their presence seemed a natural fit for our surroundings.

Hearing their dad's voice, Matthew, Stephanie, and Kim raced to the porch. The sight of the ducklings brought delighted squeals: "Oooohhh—they're so cute!" "They're so soft!" "May I hold one?"

"Of course, but be gentle. They're probably frightened."

The kids scooped the ducklings from the floor and carried them into the living room. They stroked their backs and heads and giggled when the birds nibbled their fingers. They dubbed them "Ed" (a good, strong name for a masculine duck, don't you think?) and "Dennifer" (this is not a typo—she was *Dennifer*, not Jennifer, the Duck).

"We'll need to keep them in a safe place," said Gene. He suggested the basement sink. He rigged a heat lamp and constructed a warm makeshift nest for our baby birds.

Three weeks later the ducklings had outgrown their home and needed a new one. Gene enclosed the area under the outside stairwell using wire mesh. It was perfect. The ducks could enjoy fresh air and stretch their little wings within the safety of the cage's confines. Every day the kids freed them to waddle on the lawn and paddle in the lake. And every evening they put them back into the cage for safekeeping.

Keeping the ducks safe was very important. You see, gangs haunted our neighborhood. By daytime, furry masked bandits—raccoons—hid in the trees. By night, they roamed the yards and searched for innocent victims.

We realized the danger. Ed and Dennifer, unfortunately, did not. They grew older and larger, but not wiser. When they were small, they allowed our kids to catch them and place them in the cage before night fell. But after a while, they refused to be caught. They enjoyed their freedom too much. Perhaps they thought the cage restricted them rather than offered protection.

And so, one night, the inevitable happened: Dennifer disappeared. Ed quacked until he was hoarse, so we replaced his missing partner with Dennifer II. We hoped for the best. Unfortunately, a few nights later, both ducks vanished. When morning dawned, only a few white feathers lay scattered on the shoreline.

Poor Ed, Dennifer, and Dennifer II. They thought they knew best. What do you think?

Because Ed, Dennifer, and Dennifer II were only ducks, they didn't understand that their cage was meant for their safety. They wanted to swim and enjoy their freedom instead. That was a poor choice, but their example teaches us a good lesson.

God gives His children directions for life. He knows the dangers that lurk. He knows the devil wants to destroy us. And so He's made rules to protect us. He tells us to speak the truth. He tells us to obey our parents. He tells us to choose wise friends and to run away from temptation.

Trouble is, sometimes we act like the ducks. We think we know best. We think the rules are too strict. They make us feel as if we were in jail. We'd rather be free to do what we want, but that sometimes leads us into danger.

The next time you want to disobey God's rules, remember the ducks and don't do as they did!

Share the Wealth

Dear God, thank You for giving us rules for life. Help us follow the path of the upright because it leads away from evil. Thank You that when we follow that path, we are safe (Proverbs 16:17). Amen.

List three rules your parents have given you. How can obeying them keep you safe?

Hide a Jewel

Those who listen to instruction will prosper; those who trust the LORD will be happy (Proverbs 16:20).

The Best Book of All

Read the Clue

All Scripture is inspired by God and is useful to teach us what is true and to make us realize what is wrong in our lives. It straightens us out and teaches us to do what is right. It is God's way of preparing us in every way, fully equipped for every good thing God wants us to do (2 Timothy 3:16-17).

Discover the Treasure

Nick had attended summer camp since he was six years old. He knew the routine and assumed that the other boys in his cabin did too. He learned otherwise on the morning of the first full day of camp.

It was eleven o'clock. The kids had just finished a rowing lesson and were dragging the boats from the water onto the dock when they heard the *ding-ding, ding-ding* of the camp's brass bell.

"What's that for?" asked Joel, a camper from Nick's cabin. "It's too early for lunch."

"It's time for chapel," said Nick. He looped the rope and tied a bowline knot to hold the rowboat in place. "We'll sing some songs and watch a skit, and then a counselor will talk to us about the Bible."

Joel frowned. "The Bible? It's just an old book. Chapel must be boring. Do you want to skip it?"

"No way!" said Nick. "I wouldn't skip chapel. It's not boring at all. C'mon—you'll see."

The boys raced from the dock to an old barn nestled on a wooded hillside. They stepped inside and plopped onto hay bales. A counselor greeted them with a rowdy howdy and led several action choruses. As Nick predicted, the counselors presented a skit that drew peals of laughter from the kids.

"The Bible part comes next," whispered Nick as the speaker took his place before the group. "Get ready. This is good stuff."

"Wanna bet?" Joel said. He crossed his arms and stared at a long-legged spider tiptoeing across the floor. He tried not to listen, but he couldn't help himself. Within moments, his attention was captured by a story of a nation's slavery, a burning bush, ten miraculous plagues, an army's pursuit, and an amazing escape through the Red Sea.

Joel nudged Nick with his elbow when the speaker sat down. "Was that true?" he whispered.

"Straight from the Bible. I told you it wasn't boring. By the way, have you heard about the contest?"

"No."

"We'll memorize Bible verses. The winner receives a new Bible with his name engraved on the cover."

Joel's eyes lit up. "Is that so?"

From that day forward, Joel worked hard at memorizing the assigned verses. His efforts paid off. You should have seen him grin on the last day when his counselor congratulated him and handed him a brand-new Bible...with his name engraved on the cover.

"I loved every part of camp," Joel said as the boys boarded the bus to head home. "I learned how to row and shoot arrows and saddle a horse. But I also learned something about the Bible."

"What's that?" asked Nick.

"It's not just an old book. It's God's message to me. I can hardly wait to read it!"

Many people think the Bible is just an old book filled with old-fashioned rules. That's their opinion because they've never explored it or discovered its power for themselves. That's sad.

Really, the Bible is God's written Word and is full of power (Hebrews 4:12). He speaks to us through it just as a good friend would speak through a letter or an e-mail. He tells us how to live and teaches us the difference between right and wrong. As today's clue says, it "straightens us out and teaches us to do what is right." By reading it, we learn more about God and the promises and instructions He's given us. By obeying it, we experience life the way God meant it to be.

The Bible is anything but "just an old book." It's God's Word, and that makes it very special. I hope that, like Joel, you too can hardly wait to read it!

Share the Wealth

Dear God, thank You for giving us Your written words. They are more valuable to us than millions in gold and silver (Psalm 119:72). They remain true today, for everything serves Your plans (Psalm 119:91). Amen.

Parents, tell your children about a specific promise from God's Word and how it impacted your life by changing your direction, helping you solve a problem, or giving hope when you were dismayed. This will help them understand the Word's power.

Hide a Jewel

How sweet are your words to my taste; they are sweeter than honey (Psalm 119:103).

Right or Wrong?

Read the Clue

Hold on to what is good. Keep away from every kind of evil
(1 Thessalonians 5:21-22).

Discover the Treasure

Graham and his dad watched the television news broadcast in
disbelief. A monster hurricane had swept through Louisiana, flood-
ing city streets and knocking out electrical power. Television images
showed panicked residents trying to escape the rising water. Graham
and his dad found these scenes disturbing because of the danger these
people faced. But the broadcast also showed different pictures that the
pair found equally upsetting.

In the midst of the chaos, some residents smashed store windows
and disappeared inside. They came out minutes later carrying arm-
loads of clothing, disposable diapers, computers, televisions, and other
items. One man held a stack of blue jeans. He grinned at the camera
and held up the stash like a trophy.

"I can't believe those people are doing that!" said Graham. "They're
ransacking stores and taking stuff that doesn't belong to them. That's
stealing!"

"You're right," Dad said. "They're using this disaster to their
advantage regardless of how their actions cause others, like the store

owners, to suffer. They're choosing to do what's wrong because of selfishness."

Father and son continued watching the scenes and listening to reporters tell more details. One reporter told a story about an elderly woman who invited her neighbors to stay in her home when they could no longer remain in their own houses. Little by little, her freezer emptied as she shared food with them. She also organized a neighborhood watch to prevent nearby empty homes from being vandalized.

The TV camera captured a conversation between the reporter and the woman. "Why aren't you leaving the city?" asked the reporter. "Because this is my home," she answered. "I want to protect it. Besides that, I want to help my neighbors. Some of them have nothing left. I don't have much either, but I can share whatever I have with them."

The interview ended, and Dad turned off the TV. "What do you think of that woman's choice?" he asked.

"It's a lot different than the guy with the stolen blue jeans," said Graham.

"It certainly is," said Dad. "She could be huddling in her house and hoarding her food for herself. Instead, she's sharing both with those who have less. In the midst of this disaster, she's choosing to do what's right. She's standing on the side of good, and her decision is benefiting other people."

"Wow! One person makes a lousy choice and it hurts people. Another makes a good choice and it helps. What a difference!" said Graham.

Dad nodded. "That's for sure. The choices we make are so important that God gives us guidelines to help us make the right ones. He tells us to hold on to what is good and keep away from every kind of evil. We can be certain our actions will honor Him if we follow that simple rule."

Everyone, young and old alike, faces choices every day. Here are some examples for the younger set:

- Mom asked me to clean my room today, but I don't feel like doing it. Should I obey or pretend I didn't hear her?

- My sister is visiting at her friend's house this afternoon. Should I sneak into her room and read her journal or respect her privacy?
- My mom and dad are away this evening. Should I watch the off-limits television show or read a good book?
- The old couple next door needs someone to mow their lawn today. Should I offer to do it or go bike riding instead?
- My mom's purse is sitting on the kitchen table. Should I help myself to a few dollars or ignore it?
- My younger brother is driving me crazy. I don't want him to touch my things. Should I smack him or ask Mom for help?

Sometimes making good choices is easy. Sometimes it's not. We might want something so much that we're willing to do the wrong thing despite hurting ourselves or others in order to get it.

Whatever choices face us, God's Word will help us do what's right. Remember this advice: "Hate what is wrong. Stand on the side of good" (Romans 12:9). Ask yourself, "Am I holding on to what's good, or am I playing with evil?" Ask God to show you the right answer and to help you make choices that please Him. He'll do it!

Share the Wealth

Dear Father, thank You for teaching us how to make wise choices. Please help us hold on to what's good and keep away from every kind of evil (1 Thessalonians 5:21-22). Help us always stand on the side of good. Amen.

Read the list of choices above. Discuss what action should be taken in order to make the right choice.

Hide a Jewel

Hate what is wrong. Stand on the side of the good (Romans 12:9).

Choices

Read the Clue

Today I have given you the choice between life and death,
between blessings and curses. I call on heaven and earth to
witness the choice you make. Oh, that you would choose
life, that you and your descendants might live! Choose to
love the LORD your God and to obey him and commit yourself to him, for he is your life (Deuteronomy 30:19-20).

Discover the Treasure

"Hey, kids! Come here, quick!" called Mr. Grant. Twelve-year-old
Lane and nine-year-old Alyssa dashed from their bedrooms and joined
their father in the family room where he was watching television.

"What's up, Dad?" said Lane. "It sounded important."

"It is," said Mr. Grant. "Sit down. I want you to watch this."

The children plopped onto the floor and watched as a television
host introduced his program. "Numerous choices face us every day,"
he said. "Some are large. Others are small. But they're all important.
Today we'll speak with a woman whose twin sons are walking opposite
paths because of choices they made." He turned to an attractive, well-
dressed woman and began his interview. "How old are your sons?"

"Twenty-three," she said.

"And where are they now?"

"One is a police officer." The woman hesitated and cleared her throat. "The other is in prison."

"They're twins but living totally different lives," said the host. The woman looked sad and nodded. "Tell us—why do you think this happened?"

"It's simple," she said. "They made their own choices." She recalled taking her boys to Sunday school and church when they were small. She read Bible stories and prayed with them at bedtime. When they began attending school, she prayed with them every day before they boarded the bus. She took them to a midweek kids' club at church. She encouraged them to attend youth group when they reached their teens, but that's when the boys' paths split.

One boy chose to please God with his attitudes and actions. He spent Friday evenings at youth group and developed a habit of reading his Bible at home. He hung out with wholesome friends who knew how to have fun without alcohol and drugs. He asked his parents' advice when he had problems and followed their suggestions even when he didn't agree. He graduated from high school, worked on an uncle's construction crew for a couple of years, and pursued his dream of becoming a police officer.

His twin, however, chose a different path. He balked at attending youth group. He hung out with friends who enjoyed parties—the rowdier, the better. He left his Bible buried beneath books and magazines on his desk. He argued with his parents over nearly everything—he didn't want to hear their advice, let alone follow it. He quit high school and decided to earn fast cash by dealing drugs. His path hit a dead end when undercover agents arrested him.

"The boys' choices determined where they are today," said the host as the show ended. "Whether big or small, choices matter."

Mr. Grant turned off the television. "He's right. The importance of making wise choices can't be overstressed," he said. "The second son never planned to spend time in prison, but foolish choices led him there one step at a time."

"But not everyone who makes bad choices lands in prison," said Lane.

"You're right," said his dad. "But our choices certainly play a role in determining our future. What choices do you need to make in order to enjoy a life that pleases God?"

"Well, I want to be a baseball player someday," said Lane. "I'd better choose to practice hard."

"Good idea," said Mr. Grant. He turned to Alyssa. "How about you? How can your choices affect your life?"

"I want to be a champion figure skater someday," she said. "So I'd better choose to listen to my coach and work hard."

"You've got the right ideas," said Mr. Grant. "Choices—even little ones—are powerful. Good choices lead to life. Poor choices lead to death. I pray you'll make wise choices—those that honor God. Doing so guarantees that you'll stay on the right path—one that leads to life."

Many choices face us every day. Some are easy...

- Shall I eat cold cereal or toast for breakfast?
- Shall I wear my green hoodie or my denim jacket to school?
- Which book shall I read before falling asleep?

Others are more difficult...

- This television show interests me, but some scenes aren't appropriate. Should I continue watching it or turn it off?
- My parents don't want me hanging out with a certain group of kids. Shall I obey them or do what I want instead?
- My friends want me to try smoking pot. Should I give in or tell them to forget it?

God knows the importance of our choices. "Be careful," He seems to say. "Make wise choices—those that honor Me and obey My commands. If you do, you'll stay on the right path." Because He loves us so much, He wants us to prosper. We will if we do as He says. The choice is up to us.

Share the Wealth

Dear Father, thank You for giving us the freedom to choose

the way we want to walk. Thank You for encouraging us to choose to love You, for You are our life (Deuteronomy 30:19). Please teach us to fear You, for then we will follow the right path (Proverbs 14:2). Amen.

Read the memory verse. Name at least three evils from which we'll be safe if we follow God's path.

Hide a Jewel

The path of the upright leads away from evil; whoever follows that path is safe (Proverbs 16:17).

Choose Friends Wisely

Read the Clue

Oh, the joys of those who do not follow the advice of the wicked, or stand around with sinners, or join in with scoffers. But they delight in doing everything the LORD wants; day and night they think about his law (Psalm 1:1-2).

Discover the Treasure

Tony and Joe parked and locked their bikes outside an electronics store. Three buddies roared up and screeched to a halt beside them a moment later. "Are you ready?" one asked. Tony and Joe nodded. "Okay, then. Go inside. You know what to do. We'll wait here."

The two boys entered the store and strolled toward the aisle containing video games. Their hearts pounded. "Keep a lookout for me," said Tony. "I'll do the same for you." He stuffed a game inside his jacket while Joe scanned the aisle for store workers. He zipped his jacket to keep the game hidden. Then they reversed roles. The heist complete, the boys headed for the exit.

To their dismay, a husky store employee blocked the doorway. "Going somewhere?" he asked.

"Yeah—we're leaving," stammered Tony. "Right, Joe?"

"Uh, yeah, right," said Joe. He shoved his hands into his pockets and stared at the floor.

"Have you forgotten something?" the man said.

The boys shook their heads. "No, sir."

"Think again, fellows. You see, our store has a rule. It's simple, really. Customers need to pay for items before taking them from the premises. So you have a choice: Would you like to pay for those games, or would you like to meet the store manager?" Tony's face flushed. Joe's eyes filled with tears. "Come with me, fellows."

The employee led the boys to the manager's office. A gray-haired man sat behind a huge, paper-covered desk. He peered over his glasses when the boys entered. "Is there a problem?" he asked the employee.

"Yes, sir. The surveillance cameras caught these guys stealing video games. Ask them to unzip their jackets."

"Do it, fellas," said the manager. The boys said nothing as they unzipped their jackets and exposed the stolen goods. The man took the games and shook his head. "What's up? Why would you choose to come into my store and steal these?"

Both boys fidgeted. Tony bit his lower lip. Joe stared at the floor. "Don't make this more difficult for yourselves," said the boss. "Answer my question."

Tony spoke first. "Sir, we've never stolen anything before. Honest. And we don't even want these games. But someone made us do it. Right, Joe?"

"Right."

The boss raised his eyebrows. "And who might that be?"

"A group of guys at school. They say no one can hang out with them unless they steal a video game."

The manager shook his head. "Kids, you need to understand two things. First, stealing is wrong. And second, you're hanging out with the wrong people. Those boys obviously aren't a good influence. If they were, you wouldn't be sitting in my office right now."

The manager motioned for the boys to sit. He placed his elbows on the table and leaned toward them. "I want to tell you something very important," he said. "You're headed for big trouble unless you end that friendship. True friends build up each other. They help make each other better people. They don't encourage others to make lousy choices and do what's wrong. Do you understand?"

Both boys nodded.

"Good. Now give me your parents' phone numbers, please. We'll have a little chat and decide how to handle this situation. In the meantime, take my words seriously and find new friends."

The store manager spoke wise words to Tony and Joe. In fact, his counsel comes directly from God's Word. Do you see the similarity between today's clue and his words?

Like the manager's counsel, today's clue warns us against following the advice of the wicked, standing around with sinners, and joining in with scoffers. God isn't telling us to ignore sinners, but He's saying that we're not to spend a lot of time with them, listening to their advice and doing what they do. The reason for this advice is this: If we choose bad friends, their attitudes and actions will influence us negatively.

God wants His children to be positive influences in the world. In order for that to happen, we're to delight in doing what He wants us to do. That's difficult to do if we've surrounded ourselves with negative examples.

Be careful to choose friends wisely. Choose friends who will help you become a better person, one who loves Jesus and obeys His words.

Share the Wealth

> Dear Lord, thank You for promising joy to those who don't follow the advice of the wicked, or stand around with sinners, or join in with scoffers. Please help us choose our friends wisely. Give us friends who delight in doing everything You want, and help us be that type of friend to others (Psalm 1:1-3). Amen.

Psalm 1:6 says, "For the LORD watches over the path of the godly, but the path of the wicked leads to destruction." According to this verse, what happens when we follow the path of sinners? What path would you rather follow?

Hide a Jewel

Whoever walks with the wise will become wise; whoever walks with fools will suffer harm (Proverbs 13:20).

Outside or Inside?

But the LORD said to Samuel, "Don't judge by his appearance or height, for I have rejected him. The LORD doesn't make decisions the way you do! People judge by outward appearance, but the LORD looks at a person's thoughts and intentions (1 Samuel 16:7).

Discover the Treasure

Caitlin *loved* attending her older brother's soccer practices. She sat in the bleachers at least three times a week to watch the players kick and pass the ball. Some classmates thought she'd become a soccer fanatic, but the truth was that she didn't actually enjoy the sport. She would have been happy doing other activities with her friends, but one player in particular had captured her heart.

Toby, a tall, black-haired, brown-eyed tenth-grader, mesmerized Caitlin from a distance. She'd fallen head over heels in puppy love the first time she saw him. She discovered where his locker was and knew his class schedule. She even knew where he lived.

Trouble was, Toby didn't seem to know that Caitlin existed. He never said hello. They never held a conversation. He simply went about his life, clueless about Caitlin's crush.

One afternoon while walking home from soccer practice, Caitlin's older brother, Allen, asked a pointed question: "What's with you? Why do you come to every practice? Do you like someone on the team, or what?"

Caitlin blushed.

"Aha! I knew it! You like someone on the team! Who is he? Tell me."

"It's Toby," whispered Caitlin.

Allen stopped and stared. "Toby? You're kidding me."

"No, I'm not kidding. He's *so* cute."

"Forget him, Caitlin," said Allen. "You don't want to get paired up with Toby."

Now it was Caitlin's turn to stop and stare. "How can you say that? He's gorgeous."

"You know nothing about him except that he has black hair and nice brown eyes. Guess what? The neighbor's dog has black hair and brown eyes too, and if you get close enough, he'll bite off your arm." Allen started walking again, leaving his sister behind wearing a wide-mouthed stare.

"I don't know what you're talking about," called Caitlin as she ran to catch up.

Allen shook his head. "I'm saying this. Toby looks good on the outside, but he's like a pit bull on the inside."

Caitlin furrowed her eyebrows. "What do you mean—a pit bull?"

"He's mean sometimes. I've seen him rip into other guys on the team when they've made a mistake. I've heard him growl at the coach, and he lacks respect for our teachers. Believe me, he's not what he appears to be."

Allen's words stunned Caitlin. The two walked in silence for a few moments. Finally Caitlin spoke. "I think I understand what you're saying. I remember my summer camp counselor quoting a Bible verse about the same idea. She said that people judge others by their outward appearance, but God doesn't do that. He looks on our hearts and our thoughts. He wants us to be beautiful on the inside, right?"

"You've got that right. That's way more important than simply looking gorgeous on the outside."

Brother and sister turned up their driveway. Caitlin bopped her brother on the arm. "Thanks for looking out for me," she said.

The verse Caitlin recalled is found in 1 Samuel 16. When God sent Samuel to find and anoint the next king, Samuel took one look at Eliab and thought, *Surely this is the LORD's anointed!* (1 Samuel 16:6).

Perhaps Eliab stood tall and straight. Perhaps he was a very handsome young man. The Bible suggests that was the case. But God immediately warned Samuel to look beyond Eliab's height and appearance. He wasn't the future king. Instead, God had chosen someone else—Eliab's youngest brother—because his thoughts and intentions pleased Him.

Outward beauty attracts people, but godly character pleases God. Valuing the wrong thing is easy, especially when television and magazines focus on one beautiful face after another. When we're tempted to adopt the world's standard, let's remember this—God values inward beauty.

Share the Wealth

> Thank You, God, for teaching us not to judge others by their appearance. Thank You for looking at a person's thoughts and intentions (1 Samuel 16:7). Help us follow Your example and value godly character rather than good looks. Amen.

Isaiah 53:2 is a prophecy about Jesus. It says, "There was nothing beautiful or majestic about his appearance, nothing to attract us to him." This teaches us that Jesus wasn't necessarily a handsome man on the outside. But how would you describe His character?

Hide a Jewel

> *Fire tests the purity of silver and gold, but the LORD tests the heart* (Proverbs 17:3).

Run for Your Life!

Read the Clue

Run from anything that stimulates youthful lust. Follow anything that makes you want to do right. Pursue faith and love and peace, and enjoy the companionship of those who call on the Lord with pure hearts (2 Timothy 2:22).

Discover the Treasure

Everyone at school said Stephen's family was rich. They owned a huge house, drove a fancy new car, and wore brand-name clothes. Rumor said they had a basketball court, a swimming pool, and a television with a super-sized screen. In fact, every bedroom supposedly had its own TV.

Travis' family owned one television, and everyone shared it in the family room. He couldn't imagine having his own TV in his own room. So when Stephen invited him to hang out at his house on Friday night, he could hardly wait to see if what he'd heard was true.

The boys played basketball for an hour and then stopped to enjoy snacks. "Let's eat them in my room," said Stephen. "Dad bought me a new TV last week. We can check it out. If we're lucky, there might be a good show." He ushered Travis up a winding staircase and down a hallway. "Here it is," he said. "Step right in." He shut the door behind them.

Stephen flicked from one channel to another before making his choice. "This one always has good movies," he said, shoving a handful of popcorn in his mouth.

Travis immediately knew he was in trouble. Women wearing skimpy clothes pranced on the screen. He gawked in shock for a moment. A little voice in his head whispered, *Go ahead! It's okay. Watch it.* But another little voice said, *Don't do it. This is wrong. Get out of here!* Travis closed his eyes.

"What's wrong?" Stephen asked with a laugh. "Haven't you ever seen a show like this?"

"Nope. And I'm not about to start." Travis stood to his feet and fumbled his way toward the door without opening his eyes.

"Hey—don't leave," said Stephen. "This show will be over in a few minutes and something else will come on. Just wait."

"No, I won't do that," said Travis. He felt for the doorknob. "Thanks for the basketball game and snacks."

"Whatever." Stephen shrugged and stayed glued to his seat as Travis left the room and closed the door behind him.

Several days later Travis told his youth pastor about the incident. "Way to go," said his pastor. "You ran from temptation, and that's a decision you'll always be glad you made. Temptation is like a giant whirlpool. Playing in it would be a dangerous thing to do. Its force would eventually suck you under. It's best to stay far from it. But if you find yourself near it, like you did when that show came on, it's best to get out fast.

"And as for Stephen...let's ask God to help him understand the importance of running for his life too."

Whirlpools are seen everyday in the water around our island. They look fascinating, but playing in them is dangerous. Sometimes they're so big that they could pull a boat down and destroy it. Wise boaters stay far from them.

The Bible tells us that the devil would love to destroy us. He does this by pulling us into temptation. He whispers, *It's okay. It's fun. You don't want to miss out, do you? Everyone else is doing it.* Does that sound familiar?

The Bible also says that God has placed His Holy Spirit within His children. He wants us to be safe from the consequences of sin, so He helps us know the difference between right and wrong. Everyone faces temptations every day. But we don't have to give in. Instead, we can ask God to give us the strength we need to say no, and then we can run for our lives!

Share the Wealth

Dear Father, thank You for giving us the Holy Spirit, who gives us strength to stand against evil desires. Thank You for promising that when we resist the devil, he will flee from us (James 4:5-7). Please make us strong and give us the desire to escape. Amen.

In what ways does the devil tempt you? How should you handle that?

Hide a Jewel

Don't let us yield to temptation, but deliver us from the evil one (Matthew 6:13).

A Sweet Conscience

Read the Clue

Cling tightly to your faith in Christ, and always keep your conscience clear. For some people have deliberately violated their consciences; as a result, their faith has been shipwrecked (1 Timothy 1:19).

Discover the Treasure

Jaimee craved candy—chocolate bars, licorice, jelly beans, bubble gum, and more. Sweets of every sort tickled her taste buds. In fact, Jaimee loved candy so much that she bought one or two treats every day. But her habit cost money, and that presented a problem. Jaimee received a small monthly allowance, but it wasn't enough to pay for everything she wanted to buy.

One evening Jaimee opened her piggy bank. To her dismay, only a few nickels and dimes fell out and landed on her bed. *Humph. I thought I had more money than this. What can I do?* she wondered.

That's easy, whispered a small voice inside. *Look in your mom's purse.*

The thought startled Jaimee. *I can't do that! Mom's purse is private.*

Go ahead. It's okay. She has lots of coins. She won't notice if you take a few.

Jaimee sat on her bed for a minute and considered the suggestion. *It's true—Mom won't notice. Besides, she probably wouldn't care anyway.* She glanced down the hall and saw her mom talking on the phone. She tiptoed into her mom's bedroom, found her purse, and snatched several coins from her wallet. She replaced the purse where she'd found it and returned to her room.

Later that night, Jaimee knelt by her bed to say her bedtime prayer. "Now I lay me down to sleep..."

Suddenly a quiet voice interrupted her thoughts. *Stealing money from your mom's purse was wrong.*

Jaimee stopped short and looked around. *Who said that?* Her heart started pounding. Seeing no one, she returned to her prayer: "I pray the Lord my soul to keep..."

Return the coins. Tell your mom what you've done.

Jaimee gasped. *I can't do that! Mom will be angry with me. I'll be in big trouble!*

Don't argue.

But...

Just do it.

Jaimee stayed on her knees for several minutes, afraid to do as the little voice commanded. She tried reasoning. She tried arguing. But nothing worked. Something didn't feel right in her heart and head. She knew she couldn't be happy until she obeyed. Standing to her feet, she walked to the living room, where her mom was reading a book. "Mom, I need to tell you something," she said.

"Go ahead, Sweetie," her mom said. She patted the couch beside her. "Come, sit with me."

Jaimee crossed the floor and sat beside her mom. She reached into the pocket of her robe and withdrew the coins as she spilled the entire story. "I'm sorry," she said. "What I did was wrong."

Mother hugged daughter. "No doubt about it—stealing is wrong. But I'm thankful for your guilty conscience, and I'm glad you listened to it. Now you have nothing to hide from me, and you'll enjoy a clear conscience instead."

"A clear conscience is sweet," said Jaimee. She grinned and added, "Almost as sweet as a candy bar."

God has given all of us a conscience to help us know the difference between right and wrong. When we sin, we feel guilty. That's God's way of prompting us to confess our sin and make things right. But when we ignore our conscience and continue doing wrong, it grows weaker and weaker. It eventually stops working properly, enabling us to do bad things without feeling guilty. God's Word says a person's faith is shipwrecked, or destroyed, when that happens.

That's not the way God wants us to live. When our conscience tells us we've done something wrong, we're to pay attention. We're to confess our sin and make things right as fast as possible just as Jaimee did. Doing so keeps our faith from being shipwrecked.

When we've done wrong and our conscience urges us to make things right, let's do it immediately. A clear conscience is sweet!

Share the Wealth

> Dear God, thank You for placing a conscience within every person. Please help us cling tightly to our faith and always keep our conscience clear (1 Timothy 1:19). Amen.

Have you ever had a guilty conscience? Why? How did your conscience feel when you made things right?

Hide a Jewel

> *I always try to maintain a clear conscience before God and everyone else* (Acts 24:16).

Follow the Leader

Read the Clue

Dear friend, don't let this bad example influence you. Follow only what is good. Remember that those who do good prove that they are God's children, and those who do evil prove that they do not know God (3 John 11).

Discover the Treasure

Brandon and his three buddies straddled their bikes as they sipped ice-cold sodas. Sweat trickled down their foreheads and backs. "That last ride was great, but I'm finished for the day," said Brandon. "It's too hot to ride again. I think I'll go home and crash."

"Me too," said one fellow.

"Me three," said another.

Denny scowled. "Aw, c'mon. It's only two o'clock," he said. "I'll be bored if I go home now." He swiped the sweat from his face, slurped his remaining soda, and smacked his lips. "I have an idea—let's go tubing down the river."

The other boys forgot about their drinks and gawked at him. "You're kidding, right?" said Brandon.

"Of course not," Denny said. "Look at us. We stink. Tubing down the river would cool us off."

"I agree with the stinky part, but I'd rather swim in the lake. That's a lot safer."

"You're not scared of the river, are you?" said Denny.

Brandon shrugged. "Of course not. But you know the river is off-limits. The rapids are too fast for tubing. Remember what happened to the guys who tried it last summer?" The memory made him shudder: Two high school boys had tried to shoot the rapids, but their efforts failed. The current swished and swirled and swept them downstream. It banged them against boulders and branches. Their stunt left them bruised and battered and wishing they'd obeyed the Off-Limits sign posted at the river's edge.

Denny scowled again. "They didn't know how to do it right. I do. So who's coming with me?"

"Count me out," said Brandon.

The other boys looked from Brandon to Denny and then at each other.

"Are you coming or not?" said Denny.

"We'll come," said one. He cast a nervous glance at Brandon, who shook his head in response.

"Good. Follow me," said Denny. He shoved off the curb and pedaled away with his two friends trailing him.

Brandon felt abandoned as he watched them turn a corner and disappear from view. *Maybe I am just a coward,* he thought. *Maybe Denny does know how to do it right. If that's the case, I'll miss all the fun.*

He'd nearly convinced himself to pursue them when a teacher's words came to mind: *It's okay to follow the leader so long as the leader you're following is wise.* He recalled Denny's words to his friends: "Follow me."

Where was Denny leading the boys? To the river, past the Off-Limits sign, and into the rapids.

Those aren't the actions of a wise leader, thought Brandon. *Following him would be a dumb thing to do. Dumb and dangerous.* With that thought in his mind, he tossed his soda can in the trash and set out to find someone who could stop Denny and the others before they reached the river.

Have you played follow the leader? One person leads his friends in a variety of gestures. If he hops across the room on one foot, they copy him. If he oinks like a pig, they oink too. If he pretends to sleep and snore, they mimic his actions. It's a fun game!

In real life, however, following the leader is serious business. As Brandon discovered, not all leaders are wise. Sometimes their actions are wrong. If we follow them, we land in trouble or end up with a guilty conscience.

How can we be sure we're following a good leader? By looking at his life. If he makes wise choices and pleases God with his attitude and actions, we're following the right leader. If his actions disobey God's Word, we need to steer clear the way Brandon did.

The Bible contains many stories about leaders. Some were old, some were young. Some were men, others were women. The best leaders shared one characteristic—they loved God. They obeyed Him and followed His Word.

In fact, that's the secret! When we follow a leader who follows God, we're sure to stay on the right track.

Share the Wealth

> Dear God, thank You for showing us how to live success-fully. Thank You for being a good Shepherd and leading us with Your voice (John 10:27). Help us follow You as faith-fully as sheep follow their shepherds in real life. Amen.

Today's "Hide a Jewel" says we're to live as Christ did. Complete the sentence with as many answers as possible: Christ is the best leader to follow because He... (Here's an example: Christ is the best leader to follow because He helped people who were sick.)

Hide a Jewel

> *Those who say they live in God should live their lives as Christ did* (1 John 2:6).

Stay Pure

Read the Clue

If you keep yourself pure, you will be a utensil God can use for his purpose. Your life will be clean, and you will be ready for the Master to use you for every good work (2 Timothy 2:21).

Discover the Treasure

Sixteen-year-old Celeste and her younger sister, Katrina, were standing in line at the grocery store checkout. As they waited for their turn, Katrina picked up a magazine for teenage girls. Her eyes grew wide as she flipped through its pages. "Wow—look at this headline," she said. "Drive the Boys Wild."

Celeste peeked over her sister's shoulder. Below the headline were several photos of girls wearing big smiles and teeny bathing suits. Young dreamy-eyed men draped their arms around the models' shoulders. "I wonder what they're advertising—bathing suits or bodies?" she said. She took the magazine from Katrina, turned the page, and read the next headline: "Be a First-Class Kisser." "Oh brother. That's disgusting. What are these writers trying to do—make it impossible for us to stay pure?" She closed the magazine and returned it to the rack. The moment she set it down, Katrina reached for it again.

Celeste put her hand on her sister's. "Leave it there," she said.

"I just want to read it," said Katrina. "That's not against the law, you know."

Celeste dropped her voice to a whisper. "When we leave the store, let's go for a cold drink and have a little heart-to-heart talk. In the meantime, put the magazine back, please."

Minutes later the girls were sipping chocolate milkshakes in a nearby restaurant. Katrina spoke first. "I don't understand why you wouldn't let me read that magazine," she said. "I didn't see anything wrong with it."

"I'll tell you what's wrong with it," said Celeste. "It teaches young girls how to drive the boys wild and how to be first-class kissers. God doesn't want His daughters behaving that way. He wants us to be pure. If anything teaches otherwise, we need to run from it."

Katrina shrugged. "But reading it for a few minutes won't hurt me, will it?"

"Why dabble? When we put those types of pictures and words into our minds, they're very difficult to forget." Celeste paused and sipped her milkshake.

Katrina seized the moment to ask another question. "Why is being pure such a big deal?"

"Because God says it's important," said Celeste. "He never sins, and He wants His children to follow His example. He wants us to think good thoughts and behave in a way that honors Him. When we do, He can use us for His good purposes."

"I guess being pure *is* important," said Katrina. "I want to please God. I want to follow His example. Reading a magazine like that might ruin everything, so I won't do it again."

"You're a wise girl," said Celeste. "When we get home, I'll talk to Mom about ordering a subscription to a different girls' magazine. I know of one that has interesting stories about girls who live in other countries. It has articles about things like friendship, how to dress modestly and still look cute, and how to make crafts. It even has a Bible lesson to help girls learn more about how God wants them to live. What do you think?"

Katrina's eyes lit up. "I think that sounds like a great idea. Thanks!"

Some people think being pure means not having fun. They're

mistaken! Being pure means living life as God wants us to live—pleasing Him with our thoughts and actions, and running from anything that would cause us to sin.

Some people might also think staying pure is impossible. They're mistaken too! It *is* possible. We just need to obey God's Word and follow its rules. For instance, we're to run from evil and hang on tight to what's good. That means refusing to lie and speaking the truth instead. We're to work hard and not steal. We're to use our tongue to speak encouraging words rather than to gossip. We're to love God more than anything or anyone else, and we're to ask for His forgiveness when we've disobeyed Him.

When we live like this, God uses us for His purposes. He might use our words and smiles to encourage a sick or lonely person. He might give us the opportunity to teach little children about Jesus. He might use our positive attitudes to make a tired teacher feel appreciated.

Yes, being pure is good. It's also important. And it's easy—when we obey God's Word.

Share the Wealth

Dear God, thank You for giving us Your commandments. They're right and bring joy to our hearts. They're clear and give insight to life (Psalm 19:8). Help us obey them so we can have pure hearts and see You (Matthew 5:8). Amen.

What are some of the things in the world today that make it difficult for young people to remain pure? How should God's children respond to those things?

Hide a Jewel

How can a young person stay pure? By obeying your word and following its rules (Psalm 119:9).

An Attitude of Gratitude

Read the Clue

And you will always give thanks for everything to God the Father in the name of our Lord Jesus Christ (Ephesians 5:20).

Discover the Treasure

Each morning, Megan rolled from her bed and stumbled into the shower. "Who used all the hot water?" she demanded. She sifted through her clothes closet and dresser drawers. "Look at these rags. I don't have anything decent to wear." She opened the kitchen cupboard. "Can't we buy other cereals? These are so boring."

At school, Megan whined about the lunch—too hot, too cold, too spicy, and too bland. She complained about riding the bus—too bumpy, too crowded, too noisy, too slow. And she grumbled about having too much homework and not enough time to have fun with her friends. She grumbled so much, in fact, that her friends soon stopped inviting her to join them. And then what did she do? She complained about not having friends anymore.

One day a new student, Jill, rolled into Megan's classroom—literally. If anyone had cause to grumble, Jill did. Several years prior, a drunk driver had smashed his truck into her family's car. The accident seriously injured her parents and left Jill paralyzed.

Megan watched Jill from a distance for several days. What she saw surprised her. Jill sat in a circle with the other girls her age and giggled through lunch break. She chatted with others in the hall as she wheeled herself from one class to another. She participated as much as possible in PE class. And she did everything with a smile.

Jill's good attitude irritated Megan. One day she stopped Jill after school. "So what's with you?" she asked. "Why do you always smile?"

Jill looked surprised, and then she...smiled. "I have lots of reasons," she said. "Would you like to hear them?" Without waiting for a response, she rummaged through her backpack and pulled a tattered paper from her wallet.

"'This is my 'thankful list,'" she explained, and then she began to read: "My eyes can see. My ears can hear. My hands can feel and move. I have a nice wheelchair. My parents are alive. We have a warm house. We have food to eat. I have friends. When I go to heaven, I'll walk and run again. God loves me."

Jill finished reading and looked at Megan, who squirmed in silence. "Any other questions?" Megan shook her head.

"Okay, then. But before you go, I'll let you in on a little secret." Megan leaned closer to Jill. "I felt miserable for a long time after the accident. Then I met a beautiful girl who had been paralyzed in a ski accident. She said I could either grumble about everything, or I could be grateful for all the good things in my life. It took me a while, but I finally chose to give thanks. On days when I'd rather complain than be grateful, I read the list. That's why I keep it in my wallet."

That night, Megan pondered Jill's words as she climbed into bed. Before she turned out the light, she grabbed paper and pen and began writing her own thankful list.

Having an attitude of gratitude is a challenge sometimes, especially when our problems seem giant sized. But it's *really* important. Why? Because God's Word commands it. In fact, God's Word even tells us *when* to give thanks: always. Not just when we get a fat allowance or when Mom cooks our favorite dinner. Not just when we win first place in a competition or when teachers give us good grades. We're told to give thanks *always*, even when life stinks.

Regardless of what happens, we can remember the last two points on Jill's list: If we're part of God's family, we'll spend forever with Him in heaven, and God loves us forever and ever. Those are two excellent reasons to give thanks!

Share the Wealth

Open our eyes, Lord, to see all the things for which we can be grateful. Thank You for instructing us, as Your children, to always be thankful (1 Thessalonians 5:18). Because this is the way You want us to live, we know You will enable us to do it. Amen.

List five things for which you're thankful today. Perhaps you can make this part of your bedtime routine.

Hide a Jewel

Thank God for his Son—a gift too wonderful for words! (2 Corinthians 9:15).

The *Titanic*

Read the Clue

Haughty eyes, a proud heart, and evil actions are all sin (Proverbs 21:4).

Discover the Treasure

Max swaggered into the family room, puffing his chest and flexing his muscles. His younger sister, Sheri, glanced up from the book she was reading and groaned. "What are you trying to prove?" she asked.

"I'm not trying to *prove* anything," said Max. "Wrestling championships are next week, and everyone knows I'll win. I'm just getting ready to show them what a real wrestler can do." He stopped and stared at himself in a mirror as he flexed again. "Impressive, eh? The first-place medal will look great hanging around my neck."

Sheri rolled her eyes. "I'll give you points for thinking positively. But you lose points for pride." She returned her attention to her book.

Max glared at her. "Pride? What are you talking about? I'm a good wrestler...no, I'm *great!* It's a fact. I'm unbeatable!"

Sheri sputtered. "You're wrong, Mr. Titanic."

Max's face turned red and his eyes narrowed. "You don't know what you're..."

"That's enough, Max," interrupted Dad as he entered the room. "I overheard your conversation, and I agree with Sheri. You look and

122

sound as if pride is a problem." Dad sat on the couch and motioned for Max to join him.

"Having pride means that we think more highly of ourselves than we ought to think, and that's a dangerous attitude," said Dad. "God warns us against it because He knows it can destroy us."

"Ah, Dad, I think you're exaggerating," said Max.

"You do, eh? Well, I have a story for you."

Max listened with interest as his dad told him about the famous *Titanic*. When it was built, experts claimed it was unsinkable. After all, it was the world's biggest and best ship at that time. History suggests that the captain sailed it at unsafe speeds because he wanted to show off the vessel's capabilities by setting a world record for an Atlantic crossing. His decision made it impossible to stop or change course when a watchman spotted icebergs in its path.

"But there was another possible reason for its destruction," said Max's dad. "Four days before the accident, another ship telegraphed six or seven warnings about icebergs. The *Titanic*'s telegraph operator ignored the warnings because he believed the ship was unsinkable. Instead, he demanded that other ships' telegraph operators get off the air so he could relay messages from his ship's passengers to their onshore friends. His arrogant behavior resulted in a nearby ship not hearing the *Titanic*'s radio distress signals later. If the signals had been heard, more survivors might have been rescued."

Max sat in silence for a moment when his dad finished telling the story. Then he nodded slowly and said, "I understand. You're saying that pride helped sink the *Titanic*, and it could sink me too."

"Exactly," said Dad. "Pride is bad. Humility is good. Rather than boasting about your skill as a wrestler, recognize it as a gift from God. Thank Him for giving you a strong body, do your best at the tournament, encourage your competitors, and be content with the outcome."

"I get the message," said Max. "If I want to please God, I'd better stop bragging about winning the championship."

"Do that, and I won't call you Mr. Titanic again," teased Sheri.

Max is a skillful wrestler. That's a good thing. But his being proud about his ability isn't so good. The same holds true for us whether we're skilled in playing a musical instrument or in achieving good grades or in whatever we do well. Pride causes us to forget that God gives us our physical strength and abilities. Rather than thanking Him for what He's done for us, we take the credit for our accomplishments. We say, "Look at me; see what I did." We focus the spotlight on ourselves and push God into the shadows.

When we're tempted to boast about our abilities, let's remember the *Titanic*. We need to give God the spotlight by recognizing that He gives us our special abilities. That shows humility, and that pleases Him.

Share the Wealth

Dear God, thank You that when Jesus came to earth, He made Himself as nothing rather than clinging to His rights as God. He could have boasted about His power, but He chose not to. Please help us to follow His example and walk in humility (Philippians 2:5-7). Amen.

Name the special skills and abilities your family members have. Take turns thanking God for them and ask Him to guard your hearts from pride.

Hide a Jewel

Pride goes before destruction, and haughtiness before a fall (Proverbs 16:18).

Banish Boasting

Read the Clue

If you are wise and understand God's ways, live a life of steady goodness so that only good deeds will pour forth. And if you don't brag about the good you do, then you will be truly wise! (James 3:13).

Discover the Treasure

Anika loved doing good deeds. When a single mom at church asked for someone to babysit her children for a couple of hours, she offered to do it. When the neighborhood grandma asked for help weeding her flower garden, she rushed to the rescue. When her teacher asked for assistance decorating the classroom, she raised her hand. "I'll do it," she said with a mile-wide grin.

Anika's willingness to help others was commendable, but there was only one little problem: she bragged nonstop about her good deeds. One evening she rambled on with her best friend, Ginger.

"Guess what *I* did on Saturday afternoon?" Anika said. She wrapped and twirled a strand of hair around her pointer finger as she waited for an answer.

Anika's boasting was nothing new for Ginger. She rolled her eyes and shook her head before answering. "You probably..."

Anika interrupted before Ginger completed her sentence. "I saved Mrs. Snyder's life."

"You did what?"

"I saved Mrs. Snyder's life."

Ginger snickered. "I don't think so."

"Yes, I did. The old lady was standing on a corner and trying to cross the street, but cars wouldn't stop for her. I walked beside her and helped her cross safely. She could have been run over, you know. I saved her life."

"Whatever you say," said Ginger.

"And after that, I cleaned the whole house for my mom. She has the flu, so I dusted and vacuumed. The house looked better than when she cleans it."

"And I suppose you told her so?"

"Yep. I wanted her to know that I did a great job."

Ginger shook her head again. "Anika, may I tell you something?"

"Sure, anything."

"I don't know anyone who helps others as often as you do. I admire you for doing that," said Ginger. "But boasting about it ruins everything."

"What do you mean—boasting?"

"Think about it, Anika. Whenever you do something kind for someone, you brag about it. You tell anyone who will listen, and often you exaggerate. You sound as though you think you're better than everyone else. You know what that is? Pride."

Anika was silent for a moment as Ginger's words sunk in. "I never thought about it that way, but I understand what you're saying. What should I do instead? Any suggestions?"

"Well, keep on doing your good deeds, but don't go around bragging about them to make yourself look better than anyone else. Just do them because that pleases God."

Anika thanked Ginger for her honesty. "My mom's sick with the flu, but she's probably sick of my bragging too. I think I owe her an apology for my comment about her housecleaning."

"That would be nice," Ginger said.

When Jesus lived on the earth, He did more good deeds than we will ever know. Despite His countless kind acts, the Bible has no record of Him making boastful comments about them. He never said, "Hey, everyone! Guess what *I* did today? Just so you know, I healed a crippled man and a leper. And after that, I saved a woman's life and gave sight to a blind man. Then I cast out a demon that the disciples couldn't deal with properly. Pretty good, eh?"

Even though Jesus *was* far better than anyone else, He steered clear of boastful speech. He never acted proud of the kindnesses He showed or the miracles He performed for others. He did these things because He loved people, and He displayed a humble attitude about them. He wants us to do the same. The Bible makes it very clear—we're to be wise and understand God's ways, and that includes doing lots of good deeds without bragging about them.

Share the Wealth

> Dear God, thank You for telling us what You expect from us. Help us live so good deeds pour from us. Then put a seal on our lips to keep us from bragging about the good we do (James 3:13). Amen.

Why does God tell us not to brag about doing good deeds? Have you ever listened to someone boast? Did you enjoy listening? Why or why not?

Hide a Jewel

> *Anyone who loves to quarrel loves sin; anyone who speaks boastfully invites disaster* (Proverbs 17:19).

The Wish List

Read the Clue

The desires of lazy people will be their ruin, for their hands refuse to work. They are always greedy for more, while the godly love to give! (Proverbs 21:26).

Discover the Treasure

With only two weeks remaining before Christmas, Shana sat at the kitchen table and scribbled her wish list: MP3 player, cell phone, Xbox 360, jeans, purse, new jacket. She thought for a few moments and added three or four more items. When she finished, she placed it on the counter beside the coffeemaker. That's where her mom would be sure to see it when she returned from work.

Later that evening, Shana sprawled on the couch and began reading a book. Minutes later, her mom entered the living room and sat down. "Well, my dear daughter," she said. "I read your wish list."

Shana tossed her book aside. "What do you think?" she asked. Without giving her mom a chance to respond, she began talking in high speed. "I really need those things. Everyone else at school has MP3 players. I'm the only one without. And all my friends have their own cell phones. And everyone else is getting an Xbox. Can you buy me those things? After all, it *is* Christmas."

Shana's mom looked thoughtful. "Let's backtrack for a moment," she said. She placed the wish list on the coffee table between them. "Look closely at the items you've asked for."

The girl did as her mother asked. "It looks good. I remembered everything."

Shana's mom laughed. "That's not what I meant. I want you to reevaluate. You say you really *need* these things. That statement isn't totally correct. You don't really *need* them—you just *want* them. Would you agree?"

"I...uh...I guess so."

"Can you live without them?"

Shock spread across Shana's face. "Are you kidding?"

"Think again, please."

"Uh...I guess so."

"Good, because I have a suggestion for this year's Christmas. Tell me what you think."

Shana listened with interest as her mom spoke about several organizations working to help people living in poverty overseas. "These ministries have lots of ideas to help needy people in practical ways," she said.

"Like what?"

"Well, they say a money gift can buy a goat or several chickens for a family. If a family has chickens, for instance, they can sell the eggs for income to pay other expenses. If they have a goat, they can drink its milk. They can breed it with another goat and raise the animals for meat or for the market." She paused for a moment and then posed a question. "Rather than getting lots of presents this year, how would you feel about giving a gift to a family with real needs?"

Shana recalled scenes she'd seen on television—hungry children wearing rags, mothers cradling bony babies. Then she thought of her closet brimming with nice clothes and her bedroom filled with gadgets and gizmos of every description. She looked at her wish list once more. *Do I really need more stuff?* she wondered. It didn't take long to reach an answer.

"You're right, Mom," she said. "Let's do it! Let's give a gift to a family overseas." A sense of excitement filled her heart as she spoke the words.

Shana's mom smiled. "I'm proud of you," she said. "You'll still find a gift under the tree on Christmas morning, but the best gift of all will be the joy that comes from giving rather than getting."

When I was a kid, I studied the Sears Christmas catalog and drooled over dolls that walked and talked (with a little help from their owners, of course). I wrote a wish list of all the latest toys and fancy stuff the same way Shana did. Maybe you've done the same thing.

Writing a wish list is fine so long as we don't focus only on ourselves and the things we want to receive. You see, God has a better way for us to live—He wants us to focus on others and what we can give to them rather than what we can gain from them.

Why is that so important to God? Because He loves people. He shows His love by giving good gifts to them. In fact, the Bible says He loves people so much that He gives the gift of eternal life to all who believe Jesus died for their sins and rose from the dead three days later.

God wants His children to follow His example. He's a giving God, so we should give to others. When we do so, we feel good inside. That's one way God blesses us for doing what's right. Whether at Christmas or any other time during the year, let's remember and act on Jesus' words: "It is more blessed to give than to receive" (Acts 20:35).

Share the Wealth

> Dear God, thank You for showing us the importance of being unselfish. Help us remember that it's more blessed to give than to receive and to follow Your example by giving good gifts to other people. Amen.

Sometimes we think good gifts are those that cost lots of money, but that's not true. Presents such as a homemade card or a plate of fresh cookies are special too. What gifts can your family give to your neighbors? To a sick person from your church? To your schoolteacher?

Hide a Jewel

> *You should remember the words of the Lord Jesus: "It is more blessed to give than to receive"* (Acts 20:35).

Cash or Contentment

Read the Clue

True religion with contentment is great wealth. After all, we didn't bring anything with us when we came into the world, and we certainly cannot carry anything with us when we die. So if we have enough food and clothing, let us be content (1 Timothy 6:6-8).

Discover the Treasure

"Look at what my dad bought for me on the weekend," said Lance as he led Devon into his bedroom. He pointed at the new laptop sitting on his desk.

Devon let out a low whistle. "Wow—that's *nice.* Do you have many games on it?"

"Sure. Watch this." Lance clicked a few keys and a popular game appeared on the screen. "Let's play!"

The boys entertained themselves for a half hour before growing bored. "Let's do something else," said Lance. "We have a choice. We can ride mountain bikes, shoot baskets, or go swimming in our backyard pool."

"Swimming sounds great," said Devon.

"Let's race," said Lance. The boys dashed down the stairs, through the kitchen, and onto the pool deck. They ripped off their T-shirts and jumped into the cool water. They splashed and dived and battled with super-soaker guns until Devon realized it was nearly dinnertime. "Oops! I told Mom I'd be home by now," he said. "I'd better leave. Thanks for the fun afternoon."

Devon jumped on his bike and rode several blocks toward home. *Lance has such cool stuff,* he thought. *A new laptop, a basketball court, a backyard swimming pool.* Envy turned to frustration as he thought of his old desktop computer, the basketball hoop hanging above the garage door, and the closest match to a swimming pool—the garden sprinkler. *My stuff is never as nice or new as his. It's not fair.*

His frustrations surfaced at dinner that evening. "Lance's dad bought him a new laptop," he said to his father. "My old desktop is nothing compared to his. Why can't you buy me something nice like that? And why can't we build a basketball court or a swimming pool, or live in a big house like his?"

Devon's dad studied his son's face for a moment before speaking. "If Lance's family can afford those things and want to spend their money on them, that's their choice," he said. "Nothing is wrong with owning a big house or nice extras. But our family won't be building a bigger house or filling it with expensive toys anytime in the near future."

"Why not?" whined Devon.

"Because our house and belongings meet our needs. Granted, we don't have a pool, but we can swim in the public pool. We have everything we need and a lot more than most people in the world."

Devon shook his head. "I may have everything I need, but I don't have everything I want."

"I don't either," said his dad. "But I've learned to be content with what I *do* have. And besides, a bigger house and fancy toys would mean a bigger monthly payment, and that would mean working longer hours to cover it. I'd miss time with you. I'd rather be content with the basics than sacrifice what's more important."

Devon listened carefully to his father's words. He didn't agree, but he knew he'd have much to ponder.

What does it mean to be *content*? According to Webster's dictionary, it means "to be happy with one's lot." In other words, we're satisfied with our lives. We're not comparing ourselves to others or our belongings to theirs and feeling cheated.

Today's clue says that contentment is a fantastic quality to possess—much more valuable than possessing the things money can buy. That's true because a person who possesses contentment has inner peace. He won't be troubled with envy and frustration if other people's belongings are bigger or better than his. Besides, God knows what our needs are. Our contentment shows Him that we're satisfied with what He's given to us, and that attitude pleases Him.

Share the Wealth

Dear God, thank You for promising to provide our needs (Philippians 4:19). Thank You for promising never to fail or forsake us (Hebrews 13:5). Teach us to be content with whatever You give us, and help us to be thankful every day. Amen.

Finish this sentence with as many answers as possible: I'm thankful for...

Hide a Jewel

Stay away from the love of money; be satisfied with what you have. For God has said, "I will never fail you. I will never forsake you" (Hebrews 13:5).

Mini Muscle—Mighty Power

Read the Clue

The tongue can kill or nourish life (Proverbs 18:21).

Discover the Treasure

Saturday morning, Sandi rolled from her bed and peeked through her window blinds. The morning sun splashed its rays across the yard. *There's not a cloud in sight,* she thought. *The weather's perfect!* She threw on her favorite shorts and a striped tank top, ran a brush through her silky blonde hair, and dashed downstairs.

Sandi's parents and six-year-old sister, Ella, glanced up from the table when she breezed into the kitchen. "Good morning, everyone," she said. "I'm so glad today's finally here!" She scooped strawberry yogurt into a bowl and grabbed a banana from the fruit bowl. The moment she sat down, she gulped a big spoonful of yogurt.

"You seem to be in a hurry," said her mom.

"My friends will be here any minute," said Sandi. "Remember? We're going to the mall to shop for jeans. After that, we're riding the bus to the beach."

Ella's eyes grew big. Her spoon stopped halfway to her mouth when she heard the word *beach.* "Can I come too?"

"Nope," said Sandi. She peeled her banana and chomped into it.

"Why not?"

"Because you're just a little kid," said Sandi. "We don't want little kids hanging around with us today."

Ella's bottom lip quivered. Her eyes brimmed with tears, but her older sister didn't notice.

Sandi wiped her mouth with a napkin. "Excuse me," she said, pushing her chair back. That's when her dad cleared his throat—*"Ahem"*—in the unique way he did whenever he was about to say something super important. Sandi stopped and looked at him with a puzzled expression. "What is it?"

"We'll excuse you in a minute," said Dad, "but first you need to rethink your response to Ella."

"What? What's wrong with what I said? It's the truth," said Sandi.

"It's true—she's younger than you are, and you'd rather hang out with girls your own age," said Dad. "But the problem is, your words hurt her. Try again. This time, show respect for her feelings."

Sandi glanced at Ella. That's when she noticed the tears in her younger sister's eyes. Her heart softened; she regretted the words she'd spoken only a few moments prior. "I'm sorry for hurting you," she said. She crossed the kitchen and gave Ella a big hug. "I can't take you with me today. But would you like to go to the beach tomorrow afternoon instead?"

Ella nodded as she wiped her tears.

"Thank you, Sandi," said Dad. "Those words were much kinder. And now, if you wish, you can be excused."

Today's clue for godly living says that the tongue can either kill or nourish life. James 3:5 gives another clue. It says, "So also, the tongue is a small thing, but what enormous damage it can do."

James was right. Sandi's tongue damaged Ella's feelings and made her sad. On the other hand, Sandi's tongue nourished life when she used it to speak with respect. Ella felt loved and special again.

Sometimes making the tongue behave takes a lot of effort. For instance, when a younger brother pesters you, you might feel tempted to use that mini muscle to call him nasty names. But that wouldn't fix the problem, would it? Instead of calling him bad names, use your tongue to speak kind words.

Here's another example: When you hear a classmate poking fun or gossiping about a less popular student, use your tongue to come to that student's defense. Let your tongue speak words that build up others rather than tear them down.

The tongue is only a little muscle, but it wields a lot of power. Let's use it in a way that pleases God.

Share the Wealth

Father, thank You for showing us the power our tongue possesses. Help us use our tongue not to harm anyone, but to love others and encourage life (Proverbs 18:21). Amen.

Use your tongue to nourish life within your family. Tell your folks and your siblings something you appreciate about them.

Hide a Jewel

Those who control their tongue will have a long life; a quick retort can ruin everything (Proverbs 13:3).

Soup and Strangers

Read the Clue

When God's children are in need, be the one to help them
out. And get into the habit of inviting guests home for
dinner or, if they need lodging, for the night (Romans
12:13).

Discover the Treasure

A grey-haired woman slid into the pew beside Ian moments before
the Sunday morning service began. She wore an old-fashioned navy
blue dress. A brown sweater, saggy from countless washings, covered
her shoulders. *She looks like a homeless person,* thought Ian. *I don't
want to sit too close. Maybe she has cooties.*

Ian sat as still as a stone statue for the next hour lest he accidentally
touch the woman. At long last the pastor prayed and dismissed the
congregation. *Whew! I survived,* thought Ian as the lady stood and
stepped into the aisle.

A half hour later, the doorbell rang as his mom was preparing the
family's lunch. "Ian, would you please answer that?" called his mom
from the kitchen.

"Sure." Ian threw open the door. His jaw dropped. *I must be having
a nightmare!* he thought. There, on his doorstep, stood the old woman.
Same old blue dress. Same saggy brown sweater.

"Hello, young man," she said with a warm smile. "Your mother invited me for lunch."

Ian just stared. *This can't be happening!*

"May I come in?"

Ian stepped aside, speechless, as the woman entered the house. "Is that you, Mary?" called his mother.

"Yes, dearie," said the woman.

"Come in, come in."

Mary shuffled into the kitchen. Ian's mother hugged her. "I'm so glad we met after church and that you accepted my invitation to join our family today."

Ian's mom ladled soup into bowls and set a tray of sandwiches on the table. "Lunch is served!" she called. Moments later the family was enjoying their meal. But they were relishing Mary's company even more.

Ian listened spellbound as Mary told story after story about her adventures growing up as a missionary kid in India. She wove tales of riding on elephants, watching cobras dance, and eating rice and curry. She talked of wild monkeys, ox-drawn carts, and peddlers selling fruit on the streets. She spoke about meeting and marrying a handsome young man. Her eyes grew misty as she told about the illness that claimed his life a year later.

"That was a difficult time," said Mary. "I thought my heart would break. But God was with me, and He made me strong." Then she launched into stories about founding an orphanage and of trusting God to provide food and clothing for the children.

"Those were challenging days too," she recalled with a faraway look in her eyes. "But every minute was worth it. Many Indian boys and girls learned about Jesus' love for them. That orphanage is still operating, you know. I visit it every year."

The family sat in silence, awestruck at this precious woman's love for the children and for Christ. More stories followed dessert. The afternoon passed too quickly, and Mary rose to leave.

"We were honored to have you in our home. We hope you can come again," said Ian's mom as she walked Mary to the door. Ian tagged behind.

"I'd love to," said Mary. She turned to Ian and winked. "Have a nice day, lad," she said, her eyes sparkling.

Ian returned the wink. "I hope you come again," he said. And he meant it.

Ian's mom understands today's clue. She introduced herself to a stranger after church and invited her to join their family for lunch. It was a simple act of kindness—one that didn't require much fuss or preparation—and her family was blessed as a result. Ian, especially, learned a valuable lesson about not judging strangers by their appearance. As he listened to Mary's stories, he caught a glimpse of her kind heart and love for Jesus.

God loves people. And He wants His children to show His love to others, especially strangers, through kindness. Think of ways to show kindness to kids you don't know at school or in church. Invite a new classmate to your home or to a midweek kids' club at church or Sunday school. When you do, you might be pleasantly surprised as you get to know him or her.

Share the Wealth

Dear God, thank You for encouraging us to show hospitality to strangers (Hebrews 13:2). Open our eyes and hearts to those folks we don't know, and love them through us. Amen.

Moms and dads, plan an easy lunch—soup in a crockpot and grilled cheese sandwiches, for example. Invite the children to help bake cookies for dessert. Look for visitors at church next Sunday and invite them to join your family for lunch.

Hide a Jewel

Don't forget to show hospitality to strangers, for some who have done this have entertained angels without realizing it! (Hebrews 13:2).

Good Deeds

Read the Clue

Dear brothers and sisters, what's the use of saying you have
faith if you don't prove it with your actions? That kind of
faith can't save anyone (James 2:14).

Discover the Treasure

"Let's give a warm welcome to Dan and Corinna Thomas, our missionaries from the Philippines," said the minister. The congregation
applauded as the couple approached the podium.

"Hello," said Mr. Thomas. "We're happy to be here this morning."

Oh brother, thought Marnie. *I wish I could say the same thing.* She
cast a backward glance at the clock on the wall. *It's only 11:15. I hope I
can last another 45 minutes.* She crossed her arms and slouched in the
pew as Mr. Thomas launched into a PowerPoint presentation of the
work he and his wife were doing among the poor overseas.

The screen flashed images of children with dirty clothes and runny
noses. It showed pictures of families living in rough wooden shacks
with corrugated tin roofs. It displayed photos of youngsters, some
begging for handouts from passersby on city sidewalks and others
searching for food in the stench of steaming garbage heaps.

Yuck! How can anyone live like that? thought Marnie. *How could
people be so poor and hungry that they would want to eat other people's*

garbage? The presentation continued. Before long, Marnie was sitting up straight, listening and watching with increasing interest.

"We hope these pictures help you understand the needs in that country," said Mr. Thomas when the presentation ended. "We believe God wants us to help these men, women, and children. Most need food and clothing. Many need jobs and medical care and education. But they all need to know about Jesus and His love for them. If you're a follower of Jesus, then use this opportunity to prove your faith with action. Help us meet those needs. Regardless of how young or old you are, you can help in practical ways." He listed several options. One caught Marnie's attention.

Toothpaste, toothbrushes, soap, and combs—I can send some with Mr. and Mrs. Thomas to give away when they return to the Philippines! Marnie could hardly wait for the service to end, but not because she was bored. Instead, she wanted to tell her idea to her mom and ask her to take her shopping.

"I was thinking the same thing," her mom said. "Mr. Thomas was right—this is an opportunity to prove our faith with our actions." They drove to a nearby store, filled a shopping basket, and returned to the church where they gave the items to Mr. and Mrs. Thomas. Then her mom wrote a check and handed it to the missionaries. "Use this to buy food or other supplies for those with whom you work," she said. "I'll send a check every month."

"Thank you," said Mr. Thomas.

"No, thank *you*," said Marnie's mom. "You've challenged us today. It's easy to see presentations such as you showed this morning and then go home to a warm house and a hot lunch. But you've reminded us that simply saying we're followers of Jesus isn't enough. He wants us to prove it by our actions, by showing His love in practical ways to those in need. We'll remember the lesson and watch for other ways to prove our faith, right, Marnie?"

Marnie grinned. "Right."

Mr. Thomas reminded the congregation of a very important truth: Jesus' followers prove their faith by their deeds. We can do that in many different ways...

We can show our love for Jesus by giving money to missionaries so they can travel to other lands and tell people about Him. We can give new or like-new toys and clothing to emergency shelters for women and children who need a safe place to live or to organizations that help teenage mothers. We can donate money to organizations such as the Salvation Army so they can operate soup kitchens for homeless people. Or we can give our time to help someone, like a grandma or grandpa who needs someone to shovel snow off their sidewalk.

Simply telling others we love Jesus isn't enough. We must prove it with our actions so they too might learn to love Him.

Share the Wealth

> Dear God, thank You for teaching us that faith without good deeds is no faith at all. It's dead and useless (James 2:17). We want our faith to be alive and useful! Please make us aware of opportunities to prove our faith through our actions, and grant us obedient hearts to do those things that bring You pleasure. Amen.

List three deeds your family can do within the next month to prove your faith. Do them and discuss them afterward. Ask God to use your efforts to show His love to those who benefited.

Hide a Jewel

> *I can't see your faith if you don't have good deeds, but I will show you my faith through my good deeds* (James 2:18).

Parents and a Promise

Read the Clue

You children must always obey your parents, for this is what pleases the Lord (Colossians 3:20).

Discover the Treasure

Ding-dong.

Jana opened the door. Her friend Nanci stood on the step, her face glowing with excitement. She grabbed Jana's hands and pulled her outside.

"Quick, close the door," whispered Nanci.

Jana obeyed. "What is it?"

"Shhhhh. Not so loud. Someone might hear."

"What are you talking about?" said Jana, dropping her voice to a hush.

"Remember Eric? The cute guy in eighth grade?" said Nanci. "He's having a party at his house tomorrow night, and he's invited us!"

"A party at Eric's place?" Jana raised her eyebrows and grinned. She thought of her classmate's olive skin, black hair, and teasing brown eyes. "What time does it start?"

"Eight o'clock. Get ready for a good time—Eric's parents won't be home."

Jana's face fell. "His mom and dad won't be there? I don't think my parents will let me go."

"You don't have to do everything they say," said Nanci. She tossed her silky brown hair over one shoulder and turned to walk away. "See you tomorrow night."

Later that evening, Jana approached her dad. "I've been invited to a party at Eric's house tomorrow evening. Is it okay if I go?"

Her dad peered over his newspaper. "Who will be there?"

"Just a few friends," said Jana.

Then he asked the dreaded question: "Will his parents be there?"

Jana's face flushed. "Uh…no, they won't."

Her dad looked thoughtful for a few moments. "Thanks for telling the truth. I appreciate that," he said. Jana held her breath. She knew he wasn't finished. "However, because his folks won't be there, the answer is no, you cannot go to the party."

A strange mix of disappointment and relief swept over Jana. An argument would be pointless. She knew from experience that once Dad's mind was made up, nothing would sway it.

The next evening, Jana stayed home and watched a video while her friends partied. And that was a good thing. You see, one of the invited guests brought marijuana to share with the other guests. That was bad enough, but then three uninvited high schoolers showed up, and they brought alcohol. The party turned wild and was out of Eric's control. A fight broke out, the house was left in chaos, and neighbors called the police.

Nanci dropped by the next morning and told Jana everything. "It was ugly," she said. "You're lucky you weren't there."

"Luck has nothing to do with it," said Jana. "Let's just say my parents are smart people."

Nanci nodded. "And you were smart to do as they said."

Obeying your parents may not always be easy. I know that from experience! As a kid, I remember arguing with my parents because I didn't want to do what they said. I thought their rules were stupid. I determined to do what I wanted to do, and that sometimes landed me in trouble.

One occasion happened shortly after I'd earned my driver's license. My mom allowed me to drive the family car to school one day. "Drive straight there and straight home," she said.

That's dumb, I thought. *I'll just stop at the post office on the way to school.* Can you guess what happened? Another customer at the post office left a dent in the side of our car. Facing my mom and explaining the dent wasn't exactly fun. Thankfully, Mom forgave me, and the dent didn't cost a fortune to fix. But if I'd obeyed in the first place, we wouldn't have had a repair bill at all.

The Bible gives clear directions about the attitude children should have toward their parents. As long as your parents are not asking you to do something harmful or against the law, you're to obey them. You might not always agree with them, and that's okay, but you still have to respect them.

God has placed your parents in authority over you. They're responsible to Him for your well-being. They want what's best for you. Thank God for them, and ask Him to help you honor them.

Share the Wealth

Dear God, thank You for teaching us to honor our parents. Thank You for giving us this commandment and ending it with a promise—that those who honor their parents will live a long life, full of blessings (Ephesians 6:2-3). Help us obey this command, and we trust You to keep Your promise. Amen.

How can honoring our parents lead to a long life that's full of blessings? Parents, tell your children about an instance where this promise was fulfilled in your lives.

Hide a Jewel

Children, obey your parents because you belong to the Lord, for this is the right thing to do (Ephesians 6:1).

Remember the Ant

Read the Clue

Take a lesson from the ants, you lazybones. Learn from their ways and be wise! (Proverbs 6:6).

Discover the Treasure

Another hot summer day. Too hot to work, Ted thought. He was home alone while his mom was running errands. She'd left a to-do list for him: Mow the lawn, carry out the trash, and feed the dog. He knew that she'd expect him to finish the work before she returned, but he didn't care.

Ted dropped a half dozen ice cubes into a tall glass and opened a can of soda. He poured the soda into the glass and watched as bubbles frothed up and over the rim, spilling onto the kitchen counter. *Cool. Just like a volcano,* he thought. Without bothering to wipe up the mess, the boy turned and sauntered into the family room. He flopped on the couch, TV remote in one hand and drink in the other. And there he remained, eyes glazed, until his mom returned two hours later.

"Ted," she called. "I need your help. Would you please carry in the groceries?"

"Yeah, sure," Ted mumbled. He wiggled his bottom into a more comfortable position and stared at the television screen. Ten minutes passed.

146

"TED!" his mother called. "I need the groceries!"

"Whatever," Ted muttered. This time only his thumb moved as he flicked to another channel. Twenty minutes passed.

Ted glanced at his watch. *Hmmm…it's nearly six o'clock,* he thought. *I'm hungry.* He swaggered into the kitchen expecting to see his mom preparing dinner. Instead, she was sipping iced tea and reading a book.

"What's up?" asked Ted. "It's almost dinnertime. Are you going to cook something?"

"Yeah, sure," said his mom without looking up.

"I'm hungry."

"Whatever." Mother poured another glass of iced tea and returned to her book.

Ted gawked. His mom had never acted this way. Something was obviously very wrong. Maybe she'd suffered heat stroke. Maybe the sun had fried her brain.

Ted stared at his mom for a minute or two and then said, "Something's not right. You shouldn't be sitting around like this. You should be working."

Mom sputtered on her iced tea and laughed. "Did you hear what you just said?" she asked. She pointed at the to-do list on the table. "Remember these chores? Did you mow the lawn? Take out the trash? Feed the dog?"

"But Mom…"

"Don't even start," said Mom. "You're a healthy young man, fully able to help around the house. Believe it or not, work is a good thing. You'll feel good about yourself when you do something productive, and you'll learn important life skills." She paused, sipped her iced tea, and closed her book. "And one more thing," she said as she opened the fridge door. "Remember the ant."

"Whatever," said Ted, wearing a half-smile as he carried out the trash.

"Remember the ant"? Why did Ted's mom say that? If you've ever seen a plastic ant farm or watched an anthill outside, you'll know. Hour after hour, ants scurry back and forth. Some carry food crumbs or other objects that weigh up to 50 times their own weight. Some care for the young while others build new rooms and repair broken tunnels. Each colony has at least one queen, whose job it is just to lay eggs. Diligent little critters, the ants are, and they work without being told.

God tells us to take a lesson from the ants. We're to work hard without being told. And what happens when we do? We prosper and are satisfied.

The next time you feel like being a couch potato, remember the ant. Ask your folks to give you a job. Offer to help a younger brother or sister with the chores. Lend a hand at a senior citizen's home. When you take a lesson from the ant, you'll be delighted at the outcome!

Share the Wealth

Dear God, thank You for encouraging us to work hard and cheerfully. Please help us do our work to please You rather than simply to please people. And thank You for being a good Master who promises to reward us (Colossians 3:23-24). Amen.

What's your attitude toward doing chores? What chore can you do this week without being told?

Hide a Jewel

Lazy people want much but get little, but those who work hard will prosper and be satisfied (Proverbs 13:4).

From Little to Much

Read the Clue

Well done, my good and faithful servant. You have been faithful in handling this small amount, so now I will give you many more responsibilities. Let's celebrate together! (Matthew 25:21).

Discover the Treasure

"Here, Scamper. Come here!" Twila slapped her hand on her thigh and called again. A playful cocker spaniel dashed across the lawn carrying a red ball in its mouth. "Put it down," commanded Twila. Scamper obeyed. "Sit." The animal sat on its bottom and watched the girl with eager anticipation. "I have a treat for you," she said. Twila ducked into the house and returned with a bone. "You're such a good boy. You deserve this." Scamper snatched it from her hand and wagged his tail to say thank you in doggie dialect.

Twila watched Scamper devour his treat and smiled. She loved animals—anything furry or feathery suited her fancy. She recalled her first pet, a calico-colored guinea pig with a crippled front paw. She'd chosen the runt of the litter because she felt sorry for it at first, but with good food and exercise, it grew as fat and fast as its brothers and sisters.

"Twila!" A neighbor's voice interrupted her daydreams. "I have a question for you." Mrs. Roy, the lady who lived next door, unlatched the gate and entered the yard.

"What is it?"

"Would you consider babysitting our budgie for a week? We're going camping and need someone to give him fresh food and water."

"Sure, I'd be happy to do that!" Twila flashed a broad grin.

"Great! Come over on Saturday morning and I'll show you what to do." Mrs. Roy turned to leave, but an afterthought stopped her. "Twila, do you have plans for the summer?"

"No. I was hoping to visit my cousins out-of-state, but that didn't work out. I guess I'll just be hanging out with my friends. Why?"

Mrs. Roy's eyes sparkled as if she had a surprise. "Have you ever considered starting your own pet-sitting business? The Olsens will need someone to feed their cat while they're away for two weeks. And the Manns are looking for a reliable dog walker. You're so good with animals—you're the perfect person for those jobs. Word of mouth will travel quickly, and I'm sure other jobs would come your way. Think about it!"

"I love that idea!" said Twila. "I'll ask my mom what she thinks. Thanks for the suggestion."

When her mom returned from running errands an hour later, Twila told her about Mrs. Roy's idea. "What do you think, Mom? Should I do it? Should I start my own pet-sitting business?"

"I think it's worth consideration," said her mom. "You've always been faithful to care for your own animals. Often, when we're faithful with small responsibilities, God rewards us with more. Go ahead, offer your services to the Olsens and the Manns, and then see what happens."

Twila spoke with the neighbors and landed those jobs. True to Mrs. Roy's prediction, word of mouth spread as the summer progressed, and she gained several other pet-sitting positions. The work provided her with spending money. It gave her a greater understanding of how to care for furry and feathery friends. Best of all, it taught her an important truth—God entrusts greater responsibility to those who are faithful with little.

From guinea pigs to budgies, Twila did an excellent job of caring for animals. She was faithful in her responsibilities, and her efforts paid off. Her experience reminds me of a Bible story about a man who went on a trip. Before leaving, he gave money to three servants and told them to invest it while he was away. Two servants obeyed his orders and doubled his money before he returned. But the third dug a hole and buried his portion for safekeeping.

When the master returned, he saw what the servants had done. He praised the first two: "Well done, my good and faithful servants. You have been faithful in handling this small amount, so now I'll give you many more responsibilities. Let's celebrate together!" But the third servant showed that he wasn't interested in completing even a small task. His attitude disappointed the master and made it impossible for the boss to trust him with greater responsibilities. The first two servants received a party, but that guy received a punishment instead (Matthew 25:14-30).

Why does God care whether or not we're faithful with little tasks? Because He's faithful, and He wants us to be like Him. So when you do your chores or homework, do your best, and God will honor you.

Share the Wealth

Dear God, thank You for being faithful to us. Help us model faithfulness by doing our jobs well no matter how small they may seem. Someday we want to hear You say, "Well done, good and faithful servant…Let's celebrate together!" (Matthew 25:23). Amen.

In what little tasks or chores can we show ourselves faithful? How might doing so lead to greater responsibilities?

Hide a Jewel

To those who use well what they are given, even more will be given, and they will have an abundance. But from those who are unfaithful, even what little they have will be taken away (Matthew 25:29).

Work with Gusto!

Read the Clue

To enjoy your work and accept your lot in life—that is indeed a gift from God. People who do this rarely look with sorrow on the past, for God has given them reasons for joy (Ecclesiastes 5:19-20).

Discover the Treasure

"Mom, I saw a really cute denim jacket at the mall yesterday," said Sondra. "I have almost enough money to buy it. If I do chores around the house, will you pay me?"

Her mother, Mrs. Banks, stopped loading the dishwasher. She wiped her forehead with the back of her hand and tucked a loose strand of hair behind one ear. "Sure—we can arrange something. There's never a shortage of work around here!"

When she finished her task, Mrs. Banks wrote a list of chores. She handed the list to Sondra. "I'll give you two dollars for each job well done. That equals eight dollars," she said. "Will that make up the difference?"

Sondra nodded.

"Great! You'll earn what you need and I'll have help. Sounds like a good deal to me." Mrs. Banks reached for her purse and the car keys. "I need a few things from the grocery store. I'll be back in 45 minutes."

After her mom left, Sondra read the list and frowned. Dust the living room. *Yuck—my least favorite job.* Fold the laundry. *That's a waste of time.* Trash. *Gross!* Peel potatoes. *Why me? I don't even like potatoes.* She tossed the list aside and sat down to read her favorite novel.

Ten minutes passed. Fifteen. Twenty. Sondra glanced at the clock on the wall, sighed, and set her book aside. She scrounged through the cupboards for a dusting rag and then started working. She swiped here and there, bypassing ornaments and ignoring the coffee table. Next, she tackled the laundry. Rather than fold items neatly, however, she rolled them into fabric balls. Moving to the third chore, she emptied the trash only from the bathrooms. *Why bother emptying the trash from the kitchen?* she reasoned. *It fills up so quickly that it's not worth my effort.* And when she peeled the potatoes, she left half the peels on.

Mrs. Banks entered the house as Sondra finished her last chore. "How's it going?" she asked as she set the groceries on the counter.

"Done!" said Sondra. "If you pay me now, I can get to the store before it closes."

"Not so fast," said Mrs. Banks as she walked into the living room. "Let me do a quality check first." She ran her finger across the coffee table. "Hmmm. It looks like you forgot something," she said. Sondra shrugged. Next, she walked into the utility room. "Interesting method of folding clothes," she commented at the rolled-up fabric balls. "How's the trash situation?" She flipped open the lid on the trash can. "Not so good, I see." She glanced into the bowl on the kitchen counter and frowned at the half-peeled potatoes.

Without saying another word, Mrs. Banks opened her wallet and withdrew four dollars. She handed the bills to Sondra. "Here's your payment."

"But you said you'd pay me eight dollars."

"Actually, I said I'd pay two dollars for each job well done. Because the chores are only half-finished, I'll pay half."

"Aw, Mom…"

"If you want complete payment, do a complete job." Mrs. Banks handed the dust rag to Sondra. "Take this and try again, Sweetie. You still have time to finish before the store closes."

How would you describe Sondra's attitude toward work? Does that attitude please God? If you said no, you're correct!

God's Word tells us to serve Him enthusiastically. He wants us to put forth our best effort in whatever we do rather than doing a job halfheartedly. He wants us to work cheerfully rather than whining about our chores. He wants us to do a task thoroughly rather than lickety-split just for the sake of finishing it.

I'll tell you a little secret: When you're faced with a chore that you don't enjoy, try humming or singing or playing a CD of some upbeat praise and worship music. Doing so helps pass the time more quickly and puts a smile on your face!

Share the Wealth

Dear God, thank You for loving us enough to teach us about correct attitudes. Thank You for showing us that enjoying our work is good and right (Ecclesiastes 5:19). Please guard us from laziness and help us serve You enthusiastically in everything we do. Amen.

Try this! Volunteer to do the chore you least enjoy. Sing or play upbeat music while you do it. Tell your family how you felt afterward.

Hide a Jewel

Never be lazy in your work, but serve the Lord enthusiastically (Romans 12:11).

A Healthy Diet

Read the Clue

You must crave pure spiritual milk so that you can grow into the fullness of your salvation. Cry out for this nourishment as a baby cries for milk, now that you have had a taste of the Lord's kindness (1 Peter 2:2-3).

Discover the Treasure

Mrs. Travis packed her kids' school lunches every day. Using her imagination, she did her best to make each day's menu different from the previous. Monday's lunch, for instance, was a peanut butter and banana sandwich on whole wheat bread. An apple, a bag of carrot sticks, and a dish of strawberry yogurt completed the meal. Tuesday's lunch was cold ham and pineapple pizza, a banana, cucumber slices and dip, and a chocolate chip cookie. And so it went for several years until the day her third-grade daughter, Christiane, complained.

"I don't like sandwiches, Mom," Christiane whined. "And I'm tired of carrots and cucumbers and the other veggies you pack."

Mrs. Travis looked surprised. "Oh, really?"

Christiane nodded. "Really. And I'm bored with apples and grapes and all that stuff too."

Mrs. Travis raised her eyebrows. "Well, then, we have a little problem. What shall we do about this? Any suggestions?"

Christiane nodded again. "I'll pack my lunches. My friends do it all the time."

"That sounds like a wonderful solution," said Mrs. Travis.

The next morning, Christiane rose early to pack her lunch. *I don't want a sandwich,* she thought, scanning the pantry shelves for other ideas. *I'll eat a chocolate bar instead.* She stuffed one bar into her lunch bag. *Let me see…I don't want a banana or an apple, either. But I do want potato chips.* She pulled a handful of chips from the big bag and placed them in a zippered baggie for safekeeping. *Yum!*

Christiane peered into her lunch bag and frowned. *One candy bar and a bag of chips won't fill me up,* she thought. *I'll add three chocolate chip cookies and a big piece of banana bread.* Mission accomplished, she closed her lunch bag, stuffed it into her backpack, and returned to the kitchen. That's when her mom entered the room.

"Good morning, Sweetie," said Mrs. Travis. "Did you pack your lunch?"

"Yep."

"I'd like to see it, please," said Mrs. Travis with a smile. "I'll be the quality control expert."

"Whatever that means," said Christiane. She retrieved her lunch bag.

Mrs. Travis took a peek and whistled. "Wow—that's some lunch!"

"I like it too," said Christiane.

"Wait a minute—I didn't say I like it," said her mom. "In fact, I think it needs serious help." She removed the items one by one. "Let's try again."

Christiane's eyes lost their twinkle, and her bottom lip stuck out. "But, Mom, that's what my friends eat for lunch every day."

"Sorry—that's not a good reason to feed your body junk food. To stay healthy and strong, you need goodies such as fruits and vegetables. You're allowed one sweet treat for dessert, but not four as the main course."

Christiane wanted to protest, but she knew she shouldn't. "So will you help me make a different lunch?" she asked.

"Of course," said her mom. "And this evening, let's write menu ideas that please both you and me. What do you say?"

"Okay," said Christiane as she spread peanut butter on a slice of whole wheat bread.

Everyone knows that fresh fruits and vegetables help our bodies stay fit and strong. Dairy products like yogurt, cheese, and milk are also important for our health.

Just as our bodies depend on proper nutrition to remain physically healthy, we depend on proper spiritual food to remain spiritually healthy. We avoid spiritual junk food like inappropriate videos and television shows, off-color jokes and song lyrics, and gossip. Instead, we fill our minds with good things that help us grow more like Jesus.

How important are those good things to our spiritual health? *Very.* God's Word encourages us to crave those good things as much as a baby craves milk. That's a lot!

So be careful to watch your diet—your spiritual diet, that is. Avoid the junk that will cause you harm, and feast on the good things instead.

Share the Wealth

Dear God, thank You for giving us Your Word to help us grow spiritually. It's sweeter than honey dripping from the comb (Psalm 19:10). Thank You for promising that those who obey it will find wisdom and will have a bright future (Proverbs 24:14). Help us crave it like a baby craves milk. Amen.

Name five good things we can put into our lives to keep us spiritually strong.

Hide a Jewel

I will never forget your commandments, for you have used them to restore my joy and health (Psalm 119:93).

Words Are like Water

A person's words can be life-giving water; words of true wisdom are as refreshing as a bubbling brook (Proverbs 18:4).

Discover the Treasure

Chelsea claimed her usual seat on the school bus and settled in for the half-hour ride home. She'd scarcely opened her library book when she heard sniffles coming from the person in the seat behind her. Stealing a backward glance, she saw Monica, the eight-year-old girl who lived on her street, staring out the window and wiping a tear from her cheek.

"What's wrong?" Chelsea whispered. "Can I help you?"

Monica shook her head and continued staring out the window.

"C'mon. I don't bite," said Chelsea. "You can tell me what's wrong."

Monica glanced at the older girl. She scanned the other kids sitting in nearby seats and then leaned toward her. "Promise not to tell anyone?"

"That depends on what the problem is," said Chelsea.

Monica hesitated. She studied the girl's face for a moment, and then decided to tell her story. "There's a boy in my class who's really mean," she said. "Today at recess he said I'm stupid and ugly."

"Is that so?" said Chelsea, raising her eyebrows. She reached over the seat and took Monica's hand in hers.

"Yes! He also says I don't know how to read and I don't have any friends."

"*Can* you read?" said Chelsea.

"Yes!" exclaimed Monica. "My teacher says I've read more library books than anyone in my class."

"Do you have friends?"

"Yes! I have lots of friends. We sit together at lunch and play together at recess."

Chelsea gave Monica's hand a gentle squeeze. "Then the boy's words are wrong. I want to tell you something that's true, okay?" Monica nodded. "You're a sweetie. Every time I see you, you're smiling and cheerful. People love spending time with you. Perhaps that boy spoke those unkind words because he doesn't have many friends and he's jealous."

The bus rumbled to its first stop. Monica watched as three kids stepped off the bus and began walking down the sidewalk. She grinned and waved at them as the bus lurched forward and continued its journey. The trio smiled and waved in return.

"See? That's exactly what I'm talking about," said Chelsea. "Everyone likes you because you make them feel special. You know what else? The boy's wrong about your being stupid and ugly. Your eyes sparkle, and your smile lights up the whole bus when you get on. You're beautiful—even better than a storybook princess."

"Do you really think so?" said Monica. A smile played at the corners of her mouth.

"Nope. I don't *think* so. I *know* so. And since you're such a talented reader, how about reading me a story on the way home?"

God values people, and He wants us to treat them with respect. That includes speaking to them with words that build them up, not those that tear them down.

Our speech is powerful. Unkind words hurt people; kind words help them. In fact, the Bible compares kind words to a bubbling brook and life-giving water. Imagine, for a moment, a person who's stranded in a desert. He's parched because he hasn't had anything to drink for a day or two. Then a rescuer finds him and offers him a jug of cool, fresh water. The person guzzles half and pours the rest over his sweaty body. Nothing ever tasted so sweet or felt so refreshing!

The Bible says that our words are like that life-giving water. By speaking encouraging words to a person who feels unloved, we can reassure him that God loves him and that we do too. By speaking kind words to a friend who's feeling sad about something, we can help him know that we care about him.

When we're tempted to call someone a nasty name or hurl an insult, let's remember that God wants us to speak good words. When we obey Him, He is pleased, and we benefit too because He fills us with joy and peace.

Share the Wealth

Dear God, thank You for teaching us to use kind words. Help us choose words that are sweet like honey (Proverbs 16:24). Help us use words that give life and encouragement to those who hear (Proverbs 18:4). Amen.

Read Ephesians 4:29. What type of words does God not want us to use? What types of words does He want us to say? Why?

Hide a Jewel

Kind words are like honey—sweet to the soul and healthy for the body (Proverbs 16:24).

Squash Gossip

Read the Clue

Do not spread slanderous gossip among your people (Leviticus 19:16).

Discover the Treasure

Denyse knew something was wrong the moment she saw Anna's face. Worry had replaced the usual sparkle in her eyes, and she shuffled toward the school bus stop in slow motion.

"What's up?" Denyse asked as her friend approached.

"Mom and Dad had another argument last night," said Anna. "They yelled at each other for a long time, and then Dad left without saying goodbye. He didn't come home until early this morning. I'm afraid that one of these days they'll get a divorce."

"I'm sorry to hear that," said Denyse. She hugged Anna, and together they boarded the bus. They rode in silence and went their separate ways when the bus rolled up to the school.

At lunchtime, Denyse shared a sandwich with another friend, Alison. "So what's new?" asked Alison.

Denyse chattered about her upcoming piano recital, her weekly babysitting job, and her science project. Then she dropped her voice to a whisper. "Have you heard the latest? Anna's parents are getting a divorce."

Alison stopped chewing and stared with wide eyes. "You've gotta be kidding! That's awful! They go to my church, you know."

"I know. Alison looked so sad this morning. I didn't know what to say or do to cheer her up."

"Maybe I can invite her for an overnighter on the weekend. I'll ask my mom if that's okay," said Alison. A moment later the bell rang, signaling the end of the lunch break. "Time for class. See you later."

The next day dawned bright and sunny. Denyse strolled to the bus stop and was surprised to see Anna waiting. "Good morning," she said.

Anna glowered. "Is it?"

"What do you mean?"

"I mean this—the pastor phoned last night and asked my parents if it's true that they're getting a divorce."

"Where did he hear that?" Denyse asked.

"From you."

Denyse's jaw dropped. "No way."

"Yes, way. The pastor heard it from Alison's mom, who heard it from Alison, who heard it from you. He phoned to find out if it was true. My mom and dad aren't very happy. Sheesh, Denyse, I said I was *afraid* they would get a divorce. I didn't say they were planning one. You started a gossip chain."

Denyse's face flushed when she realized her wrongdoing. "I'm really sorry," she said. "Would you please forgive me?"

"I'll think about it," said Anna. "And in the meantime, you can be sure I won't be telling *you* any more secrets."

Have you ever played the gossip game? Several people sit in a circle or in a straight row. One person whispers a sentence or two into his neighbor's ear. That person whispers what he heard to the next, and so on, until the secret's been passed to everyone. The last person repeats the message aloud. It's often very different from when it began, and it usually draws a hearty laugh from the players.

In real life, though, gossip isn't a laughing matter. Gossip spreads rumors that hurt people's reputations. And it can damage friendships, just as it injured Denyse and Anna's friendship.

How should you handle gossip? Squash it. If someone says, "Pssst... have you heard the latest about so-and-so?" answer, "Nope. And I'm not interested in hearing it."

Be careful when you choose your friends because a gossip can make your life difficult. The Bible even says, "A gossip tells secrets, so don't hang around with someone who talks too much" (Proverbs 20:19).

When you feel tempted to spread gossip about someone, ask God to guard your mouth. He will. After all, He's the one who warns us not to gossip, and He wants us to succeed.

Share the Wealth

> Dear God, Your Word tells us how to live. One of Your rules says we shouldn't gossip about other people. Please help us obey You, for we know You will be pleased when we do. Amen.

Spend a few minutes playing the gossip game. Remember—this is just for fun! In real life, gossip isn't a laughing matter.

Hide a Jewel

> *A troublemaker plants seeds of strife; gossip separates the best of friends* (Proverbs 16:28).

Bear a Buddy's Burden

Read the Clue

Dear brothers and sisters, if another Christian is overcome by some sin, you who are godly should gently and humbly help that person back onto the right path. And be careful not to fall into the same temptation yourself. Share each other's troubles and problems, and in this way obey the law of Christ (Galatians 6:1-2).

Discover the Treasure

Shayla and Leslie had been friends forever, or so it seemed. They'd lived on the same street and attended the same school since first grade. Together they'd made mud pies, ridden bikes, played baseball, and discovered boys. They'd shared secrets and dreams, laughter and tears.

But something had changed. Their friendship had developed a chill, and Shayla felt hurt. "Talk to Leslie," her mom had suggested. "Let her know you value her friendship. Find out what's happening in her life."

Taking her mom's advice, Shayla invited Leslie to her home a few days later. Leslie hesitated at first, but Shayla insisted. "We used to hang out all the time, but that's not happening anymore. I miss being with you. Please come."

Two hours later, the girls were sitting cross-legged on Shayla's bedroom floor and sharing a bowl of buttery popcorn. That's when Shayla discovered the problem. "Marijuana?" she asked, nearly choking on her popcorn. "You smoke marijuana?"

Leslie shrugged and continued munching. "Why are you so shocked? It's no big deal, really."

Shayla suddenly lost her appetite. She wiped her hands on a napkin. "What do you mean, it's no big deal? The police officers from the drug awareness program don't agree. Neither do our parents. Neither do I."

Leslie sipped her soda. "That's your problem. Actually, you should try it sometime."

Shayla shook her head. "No way. Not interested."

"You might like it," said Leslie. A wee smile played on her lips. "It makes me feel so good. Like, I forget about all the bad stuff."

"What bad stuff?" asked Shayla.

"Aw, you don't really want to know," said Leslie. She wiped her hands on a napkin and stood up. "It's late. Time to go home."

"No, please don't leave. I *do* want to know. If you're in trouble, I want to help you."

Leslie reached for the door knob, but then stopped and turned toward Shayla. She studied her friend's face for a moment, and then returned to her place on the floor. "It's like this," she said in a whisper.

Shayla listened as Leslie told about her parents' constant fighting and recent decision to divorce. "Dad already moved out. Mom told me not to tell anyone," she said, wiping a tear from her cheek. "I didn't know what to do. Smoking marijuana makes the hurt go away."

"I'm so sorry about your folks," said Shayla. She hugged Leslie. "But I'm your friend, and I'm here for you. You don't have to go through this alone. Now that I know what's been happening, I'll pray for God to change your parents' hearts."

"And mine," said Leslie. "You're right—drugs aren't my friend, but you are. Thanks for the reminder."

Shayla's actions required a lot of courage, but they paid off. When Leslie snubbed her, she could have treated her the same way. Instead, she showed care and kindness. Because she did so, Leslie told her about her family's painful secret. That knowledge helped Shayla understand why her friend had turned to using drugs, and the two girls reestablished their friendship.

Today's clue tells us to help our Christian brothers and sisters who are caught in a sin. We're not to yell at them, or call them nasty names, or turn our backs on them. We're to gently help them back on the right path, all the while being careful not to become tangled in the same sin ourselves.

If you know someone who's doing something wrong, ask God to give you the courage to speak with him about it. Ask God to give you a gentle attitude and the right words to say. Ask Him to give that person a willingness to listen and change.

Speaking to someone caught in sin requires courage, but God will give you everything you need to do what He says. Then leave the results to Him.

Share the Wealth

> Dear God, we praise You for being merciful and gracious. You're slow to get angry and full of unfailing love (Psalm 103:8). Please help us treat others, especially those caught in sin, in the same way. Amen.

Discuss several possible scenarios. For example, what would you do if you knew that a Christian friend was watching inappropriate videos on a regular basis? What would you do if a Christian friend told you that he'd stolen something from a store? What would you do if a Christian buddy told you that he cheats on tests at school?

Hide a Jewel

> *O Lord, you are so good, so ready to forgive, so full of unfailing love for all who ask your aid* (Psalm 86:5).

Broken Bikes and Boat Models

Read the Clue

Then the king called in the man he had forgiven and said, "You evil servant! I forgave you that tremendous debt because you pleaded with me. Shouldn't you have mercy on your fellow servant, just as I had mercy on you?" (Matthew 18:32-33).

Discover the Treasure

Oh, no! I can't believe this has happened, thought Evan. Dazed, he stood to his feet and brushed dirt and gravel from his hands and legs. He inspected several scratches before turning his focus to the bike. The bike—Mr. Jackson's pride—was now a twisted heap.

I'm in big trouble, Evan thought. *Why was I so stupid?* He recalled his neighbor's request a week prior: "You're a trustworthy fellow. Would you please water our lawn and feed our cat while we're on vacation?" He'd handed Evan a house key and given him a phone number to call if an emergency arose. "Thanks for doing this. We'll be back on Friday."

It was now Friday mid afternoon. Evan had entered the Jackson's house an hour prior and seen the expensive bike parked in the garage. "I need exercise," it seemed to say. "Take me for a spin."

Evan didn't need a second invitation. He finished his chores in

167

record time, strapped on a bike helmet, and wheeled the beauty outside. He adjusted the seat, swung his leg over the bar, and zoomed
away. The ride was fantastic until that car pulled out from the intersection at the bottom of the hill. Evan swerved to avoid a collision, but in
doing so, he hit a curb instead. *Crunch!*

What will Mr. Jackson say? Evan wondered. His bottom lip began
trembling at the thought.

He didn't have to wait long to find out.

"Evan, what happened? Are you okay?" called a familiar voice.
It was Mr. Jackson. "We just pulled into town. Goodness, what happened?" He surveyed the scene and then did a double take. "Is that
my bike?"

Evan hung his head. "I'm so sorry," he said, his chin quivering. "I
was wrong to take it for a spin without your permission. I'll pay you
back. I'll do anything you want."

"Don't worry about the bike, son," said Mr. Jackson. "Let's just make
sure you don't have any broken bones."

An hour later, Evan was resting on his bed and pondering Mr.
Jackson's kind response to the situation. Despite Evan's parents' offer
to pay for the damage done, he'd adamantly refused. "There's more to
life than expensive bikes," he'd said.

That's when Evan spied the boat model he'd been working on.
"What's this?" he muttered as he crossed the room for a closer in-
spection. *Someone snapped the mast off—and I know who did it!*
"Nathan—come here!" he shouted.

Four-year-old Nathan came running. "What do you want?" he said.

"You broke my boat mast! Don't deny it—I know you did it! You're
in trouble now," Evan hissed.

Nathan's eyes grew wide. "I'm really sorry," he said. "I won't do it
again."

"You're right about that," said Evan, stepping toward him. "You're
just a little…"

"A little what?" interrupted Evan's father as he opened his office
door across the hall. "A little fellow who needs forgiveness for breaking
something that didn't belong to him?"

Evan's jaw dropped. He looked at his younger brother's frightened expression, and he hung his head for the second time that day. "You're right, Dad." His voice softened. "It's okay, Nathan. There's more to life than boat models."

Broken bikes and boat models taught Evan a valuable lesson from God's Word: We do well to treat others as we want to be treated. In his situation, Evan received mercy and forgiveness from the man whose bike he wrecked. He quickly forgot Mr. Jackson's kindness, however. When he discovered his boat model's broken mast, he wanted to punish his younger brother for the offence. Thankfully his dad interrupted him and reminded him to treat his brother with the same kindness he'd received from Mr. Jackson an hour earlier.

The same lesson applies to us. If we want our brothers and sisters to respect our privacy, we must respect theirs. If we want others to be patient with us, we must show patience. If we want others to forgive us for our wrongdoings, we must be willing to forgive them for theirs. This simple lesson is very important!

Share the Wealth

Dear Father, thank You for reminding us to treat others as we want to be treated. And thank You for showing us how to treat others. Just as You forgive us for sinning against You, please help us to forgive others when they hurt us (Matthew 6:12). Amen.

Being kind to others is easy when they're kind to us. But according to today's story, how should we respond when someone does something nasty to us?

Hide a Jewel

Do for others what you would like them to do for you. This is a summary of all that is taught in the law and the prophets (Matthew 7:12).

Motives

Read the Clue

Fire tests the purity of silver and gold, but the LORD tests the heart (Proverbs 17:3).

Discover the Treasure

Four-year-old Lyle knelt on the carpet outside his older brother's bedroom door, his nose and mouth close to the floor. "Remember my birthday! Buy me a present, please," he said in his pip-squeak voice.

"All right, all right, I'll buy you a present. Now go away," said Dean.

Two minutes later he heard a knock and another reminder. "My birthday is only five days away! Don't forget to buy me a present!"

Dean tossed his book aside. He crossed the room in two giant steps and flung the door open. "R-r-r-o-o-o-o-a-a-a-r-r-r!" he growled, holding his hands high over his head.

Lyle jumped several inches into the air. His eyes nearly popped, and he ran shrieking down the hall.

Dean smirked and returned to reading his book. Seconds later, he heard another knock. "What now?" he shouted.

To his chagrin, his dad opened the door and entered the room. "Seems there's a problem," his dad said. "Lyle adores you, but it's obvious you don't feel the same way about him."

Dean tossed his book aside for the second time in less than a minute. "I love him, but he's just a pest sometimes."

"I know all about little brothers. I had three," said his dad. "They can be challenging, but you need to show kindness. Understand?"

"I'll try," said Dean.

Five days later, the family gathered to watch the birthday boy open his gifts. Lyle giggled with delight as he unwrapped each treasure—finger paint, a water pistol, and a two-wheel bike with training wheels. Then Dean handed him a package wrapped in sparkly blue paper.

Lyle's eyes danced as he tore the paper. "Look everybody—it's a… it's a…" His voice trailed off and a puzzled expression crossed his face. "What is it?"

"It's a whoopee cushion," said Dean. "It makes funny noises when people sit on it. He grabbed the package from his brother's hands. "I've wanted one for a long time. Now I can play jokes on my friends."

"But I thought it was for me," said Lyle.

"It is," said Dean. "But you'll let me use it, right?"

Lyle shrugged, tossed the cushion aside, and focused on another gift. The boys' dad frowned but said nothing. When the party guests went into the dining room for cake and ice cream a few moments later, he drew Dean aside. "What was that about?"

"You told me to treat Lyle with kindness, so I bought him the whoopee cushion for his birthday." Dean tossed the package in the air.

His dad caught it and handed it back to him. "Good try. But because your motives aren't honest, the gift means nothing to Lyle."

"What do you mean—my motives aren't honest?" Dean sat on a recliner chair and put his feet up. "I did what you said."

"Not quite," said his dad. "If you really wanted to be kind to your brother, you would have bought a gift especially for him. Instead, you bought a gift for your own use. Lyle can sense that."

Dean looked past his dad and saw his little brother blowing out the candles on his birthday cake. Guilt poked his conscience. "I'm sorry, Dad. I never thought of it like that. I'll return the whoopee cushion tomorrow and buy Lyle something that he'll like—something especially for him."

Motives are tricky sometimes. Once upon a long time ago (way back in first grade), I became friends with a boy named Danny. I smiled at him every time he looked my way. I always tried to say nice things to him. On the outside, I appeared to be his friend. But my motives for being nice weren't honest.

Danny was the school bully. He scared the wits out of me. I chose to be nice to him, not because he needed a friend but because I didn't want him to beat me up on the playground at recess. My motives were dishonest like Dean's.

What does God's Word say about motives? It says that God knows exactly what they are. Sometimes we trick ourselves into thinking we're doing the right thing, but God knows better. Thankfully, He can show us where our motives are wrong and how we can change.

Share the Wealth

Dear God, thank You for testing our thoughts and examining our hearts. Please keep our steps on Your path so we will not waver from following You (Psalm 17:3,5). Amen.

In Matthew 2:8, King Herod asked the wise men to tell him where Jesus was so he could worship Him. Were Herod's motives honest? Why or why not? What value does God place on pure motives?

Hide a Jewel

People may think they are doing what is right, but the LORD *examines the heart* (Proverbs 21:2).

The Love List

Read the Clue

Fix your thoughts on what is true and honorable and right.
Think about things that are pure and lovely and admirable.
Think about things that are excellent and worthy of praise
(Philippians 4:8).

Discover the Treasure

Ker-thump! Bang! Thud! Julian and Patrick's dad muted the television and listened closely. *Ker-thump!* This time the light fixture swayed
and rattled.

What in the world is happening up there? he wondered. He cast
a weary glance at the ceiling as he left the couch and headed for the
stairwell. *Thud! Bang!* Reaching his sons' bedroom door, he stopped
and eased it open. Sure enough, two boys' bodies twisted and rolled
on the floor in a human knot.

"Boys—stop wrestling!" said Dad, but to no avail. Grunts and
groans filled the air. *"Boys!"* he repeated. The only response was a
muffled "Ouch! That hurts!" He crossed the room in a giant step and
grabbed two flailing arms. The fighting came to a screeching halt.

"What's going on here?" said Dad, looking from one boy to the
other.

"He's trying to boss me around," said Julian.

"And you think you're better than everyone else," argued Patrick. He scowled at his brother.

"Sons, we've been through this before," said Dad. "I'm disappointed. When are you going to learn to love and respect each other?" He motioned for them to sit on opposite beds, and he planted himself on a chair between them. "In the past, fighting has caused you to lose your allowance and certain privileges, right?" The boys nodded. "This time we're going to try something different."

Julian and Patrick squirmed.

Dad rummaged through a desk drawer and found two sheets of paper and two pencils. He handed one of each to his sons. "I want you to list the qualities you admire in each other. Put at least ten items on your list. Begin now."

Patrick winced. Julian frowned. Several minutes passed before either began writing, but Julian finally scrawled first: *My brother can run fast. He knows how to burp whenever he feels like it. He cheers for me when I hit home runs. He laughs at my stupid jokes.* He paused to think, tapping the pencil against his lips as he looked at his brother.

Meanwhile, Patrick started listing Julian's good qualities: *He doesn't get mad when I throw my stuff all over our bedroom. He teaches me how to play computer games. He likes the same TV shows as me. He draws cool pictures.* Patrick stopped writing and looked up. His eyes locked with his brother's. He smiled, and Julian smiled back.

"How many things are on your list?" asked Julian.

"Four," said Patrick.

"Same here. I'll bet I can finish first," said Julian.

"No way," said Patrick. He leaned over his paper and began writing as fast as he could: *My brother is nice to my friends. He lets me eat his dinner if he can't finish it.* Julian's pencil nearly smoked at he scribbled his thoughts on paper: *Patrick gives me the biggest desserts. He lets me play my CDs loud in our room.*

A few moments later the boys held up their completed lists. "Good job!" said their dad. "Now I want you to read them aloud to each other." Patrick read first. Julian followed. When they finished, the boys grinned and gave each other a high five.

Dad grinned too. "It looks like this solution might work," he said, "but there's one more thing I want you to do. Post your list beside your bed and leave it there. Every time you feel upset with your brother, go to that list and read it. Focus on his good qualities, and you'll be surprised at how that will help you learn to love each other. Is that a deal?"

"It's a deal," said the brothers. Julian turned to Patrick. "Wanna wrestle—just for fun this time?"

Dad chuckled. "Outside, please. And I think I'll referee."

We can easily focus on other people's faults rather than on their good qualities, but that causes us to lose patience and feel annoyed. Then, arguments and fights often follow. Focusing on other people's good qualities instead helps us learn to appreciate them and overlook the things that would otherwise bother us. Our attitudes change from annoyance to respect and yes, even love.

The next time you feel upset with a friend or family member, write a list of that person's good qualities. Do what Patrick and Julian did: Post it where you can see it often. Add new ideas as often as you can, and you'll be surprised at how easily and how much you can improve your attitude!

Share the Wealth

Dear God, thank You for teaching us that love is patient and kind. It is not rude, nor does it demand its own way. Love is not irritable and keeps no record of when it has been wronged (1 Corinthians 13:4-5). Please help us love other people in that way because doing so pleases You. Amen.

Make a list of the good qualities about your parents and brothers and sisters. Include at least five...no, ten items on your list. Have fun!

Hide a Jewel

Love is patient and kind. Love is not jealous or boastful or proud or rude. Love does not demand its own way (1 Corinthians 13:4-5).

Body Parts

Read the Clue

The human body has many parts, but the many parts make up only one body. So it is with the body of Christ (1 Corinthians 12:12).

Discover the Treasure

Thirty-five students listened to their drama teacher introduce the play she'd chosen for the school's annual theatrical production. "You'll love it," she said as she handed out the scripts. "It's a mystery filled with suspense and several surprise twists."

They paid close attention when she listed the characters and described their roles and personalities. "Choose the character you'd like to be and memorize several lines for next week's audition," she said.

Zack nudged Matt. "I think I'll try out for the detective," he said. "How about you?"

"Same," said Matt. He grinned. "May the best man win."

Throughout the day, Zack asked several other guys about their intentions. Every answer was the same: the detective. "What's the deal?" he asked one classmate. "Why do all the guys want the same part? What about the other roles? There's a janitor, a mailman, a bus driver, and a store owner...they need to be filled too."

The other fellow laughed. "You know the reason as well as anyone.

The detective is the main actor. He has the most important role. He's the star!"

Word spread about the guys' interest in the detective's character. It reached the teacher by the next morning. "I understand we have a little problem," she said to the class. "Unfortunately the mystery doesn't require 15 sleuths. We need the other characters too, or we don't have a story." The kids didn't appear convinced, so she tried again.

"Every character is equally important whether he's up front or behind the scenes. Think about it for a moment. What would happen if we had actors and actresses but no one to design props or costumes? How could we produce a quality play without sound or light technicians? And how could we let the community know about the show if our advertisers didn't exist? Do you see the big picture? Every person plays a vital role in this production."

Zack squirmed and looked at Matt. He glanced around the room at the other boys. They were squirming too. He knew the teacher was right. Each position needed to be filled, and each role was equally important for the production to be successful.

"So," the teacher continued. "Who will audition for the bus driver's part?"

Zack raised his hand.

Just as the school play required various roles to be successful, so God's family requires people with many different abilities in order to function properly. Sometimes in church we think certain individuals play a more important role than others because they're on the stage a lot, but that's not really true.

The Bible compares God's family to a body (1 Corinthians 12:12-21). A body has many parts—eyes, ears, skin, fingernails, toes, wrists, nose...The list goes on and on. Only a few parts are actually seen. The rest, like the heart and liver, are tucked inside. Each part, seen or unseen, plays an important role in our well-being. Imagine how silly our bodies would look if an ear decided it didn't like its job and changed itself to an eye. Or if an arm decided it would rather be a leg! Or if every body part decided to be a chin!

In church, just as in a human body, every part is important. Some people teach Sunday school classes. Others fold the church bulletins. Some clean the bathrooms. Others sort and file library books. Lots of important work happens behind the scenes.

What's your role in church? Perhaps you can play piano or pick up the communion cups after they've been used. Maybe you help the nursery workers care for the babies or help a Sunday school teacher who has lots of kids in her class. Perhaps you can pull weeds from the church flower beds or draw pretty cards for older folks who can't attend church anymore because of poor health.

Think of the big picture! Your role is important regardless of what it is! God's family needs *you!*

Share the Wealth

> Dear God, thank You for making people with different abilities. Thank You that everyone plays an important role in Your family. Help us to perform our tasks with joy and to encourage others as they do their work well. Help us keep harmony in the body so it functions with excellence (1 Corinthians 12:25). Amen.

What roles do your family members play in God's family? Small children might enjoy drawing a picture of their bodies. If so, post it on the fridge for all to see and enjoy.

Hide a Jewel

> *Now all of you together are Christ's body, and each one of you is a separate and necessary part of it* (1 Corinthians 12:27).

I Can Do It!

Read the Clue

Each time he said, "My gracious favor is all you need. My power works best in your weakness." So now I am glad to boast about my weaknesses, so that the power of Christ may work through me (2 Corinthians 12:9).

Discover the Treasure

"Listen up, everyone," said Mr. Parks to his seventh-grade class. "Our school will be hosting a fundraiser to raise money for new gym equipment. The organizers want the students to participate. They've asked our class to put on a talent show."

Most students expressed their approval: "All right!" "That's cool!" "I know what I can do!"

A few others groaned. "You've gotta be kidding." "That's a dumb idea." "I don't have any talent."

Myron sat quietly at his desk and listened to his classmates' responses. *That's me,* he thought. *I don't have any talent. I can't do anything.*

"Put up your hand if you'd like to play a musical instrument," said Mr. Parks. A half dozen kids raised their hands. "I'll play piano," said one. "I've been taking classical guitar lessons," said another.

"Great! Now, put up your hand if you'd like to perform a skit." Eight students responded.

"We need someone to recite a poem." One girl raised her hand.

And so the list continued. Finally the teacher said, "We have only one slot left. Who doesn't have a job yet?" He glanced around the room and then reread his notes. "Hmmm. Looks as though Myron doesn't have a job. Is that right?" He looked at the boy over his glasses.

Myron squirmed. "Yeah—that's right," he muttered.

"Well, not for long. There's one role left, and I think you'll like it. You can be the master of ceremonies. You'll lead the program by introducing each act. You can even tell funny jokes between them if you want."

You must be kidding, thought Myron. *Me? Lead a program? Introduce the others? Tell funny jokes to a crowd? I can't do that! I'd rather hide in a hole!*

The teacher sensed Myron's dismay. "You'll be a *fantastic* master of ceremonies. I'll help you prepare, and everything will be fine. You'll see."

Mr. Parks met with Myron after school on several occasions to help him organize his material and practice presenting it. He also offered him some good advice: "Pray about your role, Myron. Ask God to give you strength to do your job with excellence. He will help you."

Mr. Parks was right in more ways than one. God *did* help Myron, and Myron *was* a fantastic MC. He followed his teacher's suggestions. He memorized a few funnies to tell at the show. He practiced his lines at home. And most important of all, he asked God to help him. Granted, his stomach did somersaults when he took his place before the audience, but before long he felt comfortable and actually enjoyed himself.

When the talent show ended, Mr. Parks slapped Myron good-naturedly on the back. "Well done," he said. "That wasn't so bad, was it?"

Myron grinned. "When's the next talent show?"

At first, Myron felt as though he had no talent or ability. Did you know that Moses felt the same way? The Bible says God gave him a role—he was to lead his people out of slavery. He heard God speak, but he didn't exactly jump for joy. Instead, like Myron, he doubted his ability: "But who am I to appear before Pharaoh?...How can you expect me to lead the Israelites out of Egypt?" (Exodus 3:11). When Moses finally agreed to do what God was asking, he learned that God would give him the strength for the task.

The next time you're facing a task that seems too big for you, remember Myron and Moses. Better yet, remember God's promise to give you strength to get the job done and then do your task with gusto!

Share the Wealth

> Thank You, God, that we can do all things through Christ, who gives us strength (Philippians 4:13). When we're feeling as though a task is too big for us, please remind us that we're not alone. Thank You for being with us just as You were with Moses. Amen.

What talents do you have? What talents would you like to develop? How can you do that?

Hide a Jewel

> For I can do everything with the help of Christ who gives me the strength I need (Philippians 4:13).

Precious People

When God created people, he made them in the likeness of God. He created them male and female, and he blessed them and called them "human" (Genesis 5:1-2).

Discover the Treasure

"Mom, can I visit Mrs. King?" said Tonya. It was Tuesday afternoon and, as usual, Tonya stopped by the nursing home on her way home from school. Her mom volunteered at the facility once a week. Tonya enjoyed visiting the grandmas and grandpas while waiting for her Mom to finish her chores.

"That should be fine, unless she's having a nap," said her mother. Tonya walked down the long corridor and stopped at a door decorated by a silk floral wreath. *Beulah King*, the nameplate read. She knocked and listened. Nothing. She knocked again.

"Come in," said a feeble voice.

Tonya pushed the door open. The elderly woman was sitting in her wheelchair, gazing out the window. She turned to face the girl and flashed a puckered smile.

"Hello, dearie," said Mrs. King. "I'm so glad you've come. I miss you when you're not here."

Tonya crossed the room and gave Mrs. King a hug. "I miss you too. What mischief have you been in since I saw you last week?"

Mrs. King's eyes twinkled. "I played bingo and won," she said. "And I painted a clay dish. Put purple pansies all over it. The teacher said it looked beautiful. It's sitting over there if you want to see it."

"Of course I want to see it," said Tonya. She picked it up and studied it. "The teacher was right—it *is* beautiful. Just like you."

Mrs. King chuckled, and then her expression turned serious. "You always make me feel special. You know, some days I sit here and wonder why I'm still around. The nurses have to dress me and bathe me and brush my hair. I need someone to help feed me. I feel like such a bother. I'm not even sure why you visit me every week. You could be playing with your friends rather than sitting here."

Tonya put her hand on Mrs. King's shoulder. "I come here every week because *you're* my friend. I love hearing your stories about when you were my age. You've taught me a lot about life before television and computers. And you always have time for me."

"I'm so glad you feel that way," said Mrs. King. "Would you like a cup of tea? Perhaps you could push me into the dining room, and we can round up a nice, hot drink."

"Sounds great," said Tonya. She helped Mrs. King put her feet on the wheelchair's footrests, released the brake, and pushed her through the door and down the hall.

Twenty minutes later, Tonya's mother found the duo sipping tea and swapping stories. "I'm sorry to interrupt," she said, "but it's time to head home. It's almost five o'clock, and I still have to cook dinner for our family." Tonya said goodbye and kissed Mrs. King gently on the top of her head.

"Mrs. King tells me your visits mean more than words can say," said Tonya's mom as they drove home. "She often feels useless, but you make her feel loved and valued. I'm so proud of your willingness to visit her."

Tonya smiled. "Some kids at school don't understand why I enjoy doing it. They say the old people don't know anything, but I don't agree. I tell them they're special, and being with them is a pleasure."

"Maybe you ought to bring your friends along next week. Introduce them to Mrs. King. Let them get to know her firsthand."

"That's a great idea," said Tonya. "And maybe they'll want to adopt a grandma or grandpa too."

Tonya and her mom set a wonderful example because they recognize that human life is precious. Some folks, like Mrs. King, are confined to wheelchairs because their bodies are weak with age. Others are confined to beds because they have a serious illness. Some are born with medical problems that keep them from participating in normal everyday activities. I've heard some people say these folks don't have much to offer the rest of the world.

That's far from the truth! God's Word teaches us that human life is precious. God created men and women in His image, and they're valuable to Him. He loves them and wants others to show His love to them through kind words and deeds.

Let's make sure our thoughts about human life match God's thoughts. Let's regard life as precious and look for opportunities to share His love with others.

Share the Wealth

Dear God, thank You for regarding people as precious and for making us only a little lower than Yourself. You've crowned us with glory and honor (Psalm 8:5). Help us treat others with the same respect You show us. Amen.

List three ways your family can show that human life is precious (for example, older kids can volunteer to help in the church nursery on Sunday mornings, participate in a church service at a nursing home, and treat siblings lovingly).

Hide a Jewel

So God created people in his own image; God patterned them after himself; male and female he created them (Genesis 1:27).

A Solid Foundation

Read the Clue

Anyone who listens to my teaching and obeys me is wise,
like a person who builds a house on solid rock...But anyone
who hears my teaching and ignores it is foolish, like a person
who builds a house on sand (Matthew 7:24,26).

Discover the Treasure

Kegan's folks were out of town for the weekend. His grandparents
were staying with him, and they'd given him permission to invite a
friend over on Friday evening. Kegan chose Noah, a boy who'd moved
to his school three months prior. "Maybe we can watch a DVD," said
Kegan. "Do you have any good ones at home?"

"I'll find something," said Noah.

When Friday evening arrived, Noah handed Kegan the DVD he'd
brought. Kegan popped it into the player, grabbed the remote, and
punched the ON button. "Have you already seen this one?" he asked.

Noah shook his head. "My dad just bought it. But I saw the ad for
it on TV, and it looked really good."

For the next 20 minutes, the boys stared at the screen. Unfortunately,
the show was anything but good. One violent act followed another.
Two actors beat each other up in a fist fight. Others chased their
enemies through abandoned warehouses and down dark alleys while

shooting rounds of ammunition. Explosions burned buildings and threw cars into the air.

The action so captivated the boys' attention that they didn't notice Kegan's grandfather enter the room. He stood behind the couch where they sat. After watching the movie for several minutes, he could hold his silence no longer. "Boys," he said. "May I speak with you?"

Kegan whirled around. "Grandpa! When did you come in? Do you like the show?"

Grandpa reached for the remote and hit the PAUSE button. He sat in a chair facing the boys. "I came in a few minutes ago, and no, I don't like the show."

"But why?" said Kegan. "It has lots of action!"

"I agree with you—it has *lots* of action. The trouble is, it's not a good type of action."

A puzzled expression crossed Noah's face. "What do you mean?" he said. "We always watch DVDs like this at home. My dad says they're okay."

Grandpa shook his head. "I'm sorry, but I don't agree with your dad, and many, many other people who think the same way. It's dangerous for us to fill our minds with pictures like this movie contains."

Noah scowled. "Naw, nothing will happen."

"I wouldn't be so sure," said Grandpa. "I want to show you something." He left the room and returned carrying a table game. Opening the box, he dumped fifty-four rectangular wooden blocks on the coffee table. Then he built a tower, carefully criss-crossing the blocks in layers of three. "It looks good, doesn't it?" he said when he finished. "It's straight and strong like our lives when we build them on the foundation of God's Word. For instance, God tells us to fix our thoughts on what's true and honorable and right and lovely (Philippians 4:8). We do well when we obey by guarding what we feed our minds. But watch this."

Grandpa knocked the blocks down and rebuilt the tower. This time he laid the blocks in a haphazard fashion. "When we build our lives on whatever society says is okay rather than on the foundation of God's Word, we run into problems." He tweaked the tower with his finger. Blocks crashed to the table and bounced to the floor. "Which tower do you want your lives to look like—the strong one or the weak one?" he asked.

"The strong tower," said both boys.

"Then build them on the foundation of God's Word," said Grandpa.

"That means turning off this movie," said Kegan. He turned to Noah. "Do you mind not watching it?"

"No," said Noah, gathering the blocks into a heap. "Let's play this game instead."

Kegan's Grandpa is a wise man. He understands that God's Word teaches us right from wrong. He knows we do well when we obey it and that we suffer consequences when we don't.

Jesus said, "Anyone who listens to my teaching and obeys me is wise, like a person who builds a house on solid rock...But anyone who hears my teaching and ignores it is foolish, like a person who builds a house on sand."

Do you want to be wise? Do you want your life to be like the strong tower? Then read the Bible and ask God to help you obey His words. He has your best in mind, so He'll be happy to answer your prayer.

Share the Wealth

Dear God, thank You for giving us Your truth, which stands firm like a foundation stone (2 Timothy 2:19). Teach us to treasure it. Make it our heart's delight so we will love to obey it (Psalm 119:111). Amen.

Discuss the concept of building a house (your life) on a weak foundation versus a strong foundation. Name three behaviors that would create a weak foundation (such as taking advice from friends who think the Bible is silly). How should we behave instead?

Hide a Jewel

Some false teachers may deny these things, but these are the sound, wholesome teachings of the Lord Jesus Christ, and they are the foundation for a godly life (1 Timothy 6:3).

Truth Rules

Read the Clue

Jesus said to the people who believed in him, "You are truly my disciples if you keep obeying my teachings. And you will know the truth, and the truth will set you free" (John 8:31-32).

Discover the Treasure

Jodi burst through the door and tossed her backpack on the floor. "Aaahhh—I'm so confused!" she wailed.

Mom stopped typing and looked up from her computer. "Hello to you too my dear. You sound as though you had a *wonderful* day."

"It would have been wonderful if my friends hadn't ruined it for me." Jodi stomped to the fridge and scrounged for a snack. "They huddled together at lunch and came up with a new game." She wiped an apple on her sleeve and sat down at the table.

Mom saved her material on the computer. She poured a cup of coffee and sat down across the table from her daughter. "What's so upsetting about that?" she asked.

"Listen to this—the game is played at the mall. Everyone will meet at the entrance at three o'clock on Saturday. Then we'll split up and go into any store we choose. That's where things get tricky."

"Tricky?"

"Yes. We'll have five minutes to enter a store, take an item, and return to the entrance."

Mom frowned. "Let me get this straight. You're supposed to take something—without paying for it?"

Jodi crunched into her apple and nodded. "The winner is the person who takes the most expensive item."

"That's not a game. That's stealing," said Mom.

"That's what I told them," said Jodi, "but they laughed at me. They said it's not wrong. They said it's fun—it will test our skill. And they insisted that the store owners will never miss one little item." She groaned. "I'm so confused."

"What's confusing?" asked Mom. "It sounds pretty straightforward."

Jodi tossed her apple core in the trash and then poured a glass of milk. "Maybe I'm old-fashioned. Maybe I'm just hung up on stupid rules. Maybe it's not wrong to take something from a store, and I need to change the way I think. After all, everyone else seems to think the game is okay."

"Oh, Jodi—you're on a slippery slope," warned Mom. "You'll slide into trouble unless you stand on the truth."

"But I don't know what the truth is anymore."

Mom reached across the table for her Bible and placed it before Jodi. "God's Word is truth. What does He say about taking something that doesn't belong to us?"

"That's easy. He calls it stealing and says we shouldn't do it" (Exodus 20:15).

"Exactly. Confusion sets in when we start meddling with the truth."

"What do you mean—meddling?" said Jodi.

"Sometimes we twist the truth. We play with the wording and make it suit our purposes. Your friends don't see anything wrong with taking something that doesn't belong to them if they consider it a game or a skill-testing activity. By calling it something other than stealing, they think they can make it acceptable. They've warped the truth to excuse their sin.

"Be careful, Jodi. Others may think a certain activity is okay, but that doesn't make it right. God's Word tells us what is right, and it remains the same regardless of people's opinions or feelings. It's completely trustworthy. Follow it, and you'll never feel confused about whether a certain activity is right or wrong."

Jodi poured another glass of milk. She drank it slowly, pondering the words she'd heard. "Thanks, Mom. I'll try to tell these things to the girls tomorrow. If they won't listen, I'll make other plans for Saturday."

God's Word contains the instructions for living life successfully. If we regard those instructions as truth, confusion will never be a problem for us. Jesus said so when He encouraged His followers to obey His teachings. He said that if we obey what He's taught us, we'll know the truth, and the truth will set us free.

Because God never changes, His Word remains true forever. Isn't that cool? We never have to worry that His words will be true one day and false the next. And they will always, always, always help us know the difference between right and wrong.

Share the Wealth

Dear God, we praise You because You are near, and all Your commands are true (Psalm 119:151). Send out Your light and truth—let them guide us to the place where You live (Psalm 43:3). We love You. Amen.

Hide a Jewel

The word of the LORD holds true, and everything he does is worthy of our trust (Psalm 33:4).

Piano Recitals
and Lessons in Love

Read the Clue

See how very much our heavenly Father loves us, for he allows us to be called his children, and we really are! (1 John 3:1).

Discover the Treasure

"I've scheduled a recital for all my students," said my piano teacher. "Everyone's parents and friends will be invited. It will be great fun!"

Her words made my heart pound and hands sweat. *If I make a mistake, what will people think of me?* I wondered. My 13-year-old mind began plotting ways to escape the torture. *Maybe I can fake the flu. Perhaps I can just disappear—vanish into thin air without leaving a trace. I'll come back when the recital's over.*

I was still plotting my plan when my teacher spoke again. "You'll be required to memorize your recital song."

MEMORIZE? Like a hairy monster with big claws, panic seized me and hung on tight. *Who's she kidding? My song is three pages long! Impossible!*

Unfortunately, my teacher wasn't kidding. She'd made a rule, and the rule stuck. And so I worked hard. I really did. I practiced my song until I could practically play it in my dreams.

The day of the recital came. Minutes before leaving our house for the auditorium, I asked my mom and older sister to listen as I played my song—"The Olive Garden"—once more, for good measure. "Well done," they said after I struck the final note. "You're ready for tonight's performance!"

One by one the students played their songs. Finally the teacher called my name. I sat on the piano bench and focused on the ivory keys before me. I drew a deep breath and began playing. Two measures later, my worst fears came true.

My mind went blank. I searched for a mental clue but found nothing. I thought of the crowd behind me. My cheeks burned. Tears rushed to my eyes. And my teacher rushed to my rescue. Setting my piano book in front of me, she whispered, "Try again—everything will be okay," and disappeared to side stage.

It worked. I glanced at the music for a mere split second. Then, focusing once again on the keys, I played the entire song by memory. The audience clapped. I bowed. And I swore I'd never participate in another recital.

Why? Because my performance hadn't been perfect. Forgetting my song marked me as a failure, or so I thought. And who could ever love a failure? In reality, nothing was further from the truth.

Forgetting my song made me feel embarrassed, but it didn't turn me into an unlovable failure. Regardles of what happened in the recital hall, I was still God's child, and He loved me. Remembering that fact helped me get over my fear of playing the piano in public again. When I was in high school, I became my church's official pianist. And guess what? I eventually became a piano teacher and was able to encourage my students to play in public too. Believe me, I could understand their nervous feelings and fear of failure!

How about you? Have you ever felt like a failure? Perhaps you stumbled and fell while running a race at a track meet. Maybe you tried giving a speech or book report in front of your class, but your throat dried and made it nearly impossible to talk. Perhaps you offered an answer in class, but it was incorrect and kids snickered.

Maybe you sometimes feel as though you can't do anything right. You want to vanish into thin air or crawl into a hole. When that happens, you need to remember something *very* important!

God never sees His children as failures. He thinks you're special. He thinks you're awesome. He loves you more than you can ever imagine. So when your mind says you're a failure, just answer, "That's a lie. My heavenly Father loves me. He thinks I'm special. And *that's* the truth."

Share the Wealth

> Dear God, thank You for loving us more than we can imagine. Please give us the power to understand how wide, how long, how high, and how deep Your love really is. And fill us with the fullness of life and power that comes from You (Ephesians 3:18-19). Amen.

Can you recall a situation that left you feeling like a failure? How did you move beyond that feeling?

Hide a Jewel

> *Whether we are high above the sky or in the deepest ocean, nothing in all creation will ever be able to separate us from the love of God that is revealed in Christ Jesus our Lord* (Romans 8:39).

Pray Away Your Worries

Read the Clue

Don't worry about anything; instead, pray about everything. Tell God what you need, and thank him for all he has done (Philippians 4:6).

Discover the Treasure

"I'm home!" said Dionne. She tossed her backpack on the floor and hung her jacket in the closet. She listened for her mom's usual response. None came. *That's strange,* she thought. *Mom always answers. Maybe she's upstairs and didn't hear me.*

Dionne entered the kitchen and headed for the fridge. As she did, she noticed her mother standing on the outside deck beyond the sliding glass door. She was speaking on her cell phone. Her face looked pale and frightened as she wiped a tear from her cheek.

What's wrong? Dionne thought. She approached the glass door, which stood slightly ajar. Her mother's voice filtered through the crack: "I don't know what to do. We paid our bills this month, but there's no money left. And now this."

Dionne backed away from the door. She pulled out a chair at the kitchen table and sat down. *Whatever's happened, it must be serious,* she thought. She waited for what felt like eternity until her mom ended the phone call and entered the house.

She seemed startled to see Dionne. "Oh—you're home," she said. "Did you have a good day?"

"I did—until now. I overhead a few sentences, Mom. What's wrong? Something happened, and it doesn't sound good."

Her mom poured a cup of coffee and seated herself across the table from Dionne. "It's a long story, and I won't bore you with all the details. In a nutshell, Dad's boss will be laying off some workers in a month. Unfortunately, Dad is one of those workers. We suspected this might be coming, so we've been very careful to limit our spending. But do you remember what happened to the car two weeks ago?"

"Yeah—something broke in the motor."

"The transmission blew. The repairs nearly emptied our bank account. That's not all, though. Granny phoned this morning. She said Grandpa was hospitalized during the night. He's very ill; doctors don't know what's wrong. Granny thinks I should come as soon as possible. Trouble is, I'd need an airline ticket, and we can't afford it." Mom drew a deep sigh. Her shoulders drooped.

Dionne looked at her mom for a moment, but then her gaze shifted to the fridge behind her. Its door held several magnets. A Bible verse was written on one: "Don't worry about anything; instead, pray about everything. Tell God what you need, and thank him for all he has done." She smiled.

"Uh…Mom…" said Dionne. "Would you say you're worried right now?"

"Yes, I'd say that."

"Well….may I make a suggestion?"

"Go ahead."

"In the past, when I've worried about tests and friends and stuff like that, you've told me to remember God's Word. You've said He wants me to pray—to tell Him what I need because He cares about me. And you've often reminded me to thank God for everything He's done already. Your advice has helped me. Now you're the one who needs it—do you think it can help you too?"

Dionne's mom nodded. A smile crept across her face. "Out of the mouth of babes. Thanks for the reminder, kiddo. Yes, it can help me too."

Sometimes we forget that God's Word tells us how to handle worry. Dionne remembered—we're to pray. God loves us so much that He wants us to tell Him about our concerns and thank Him for the good things He's already done for us. When we do that, the scary feelings inside seem to disappear. Peace replaces them (Philippians 4:6-7).

When I was about 12 years old, my dad thought about applying for a new job in a different town. I didn't want to move and leave all my friends behind. I worried so much that I couldn't sleep at night, and an itchy rash broke out on my arms. I finally told God what I needed (peace) and thanked Him that He loved me and would look after me wherever our family lived. The worry disappeared, and so did the rash.

Next time you feel worried about something, follow the advice in God's Word. Pray. It's a sure cure.

Share the Wealth

Dear Father, thank You for inviting us to tell You what we need. Thank You for loving us so much and for filling our hearts with peace, which is far more wonderful than the human mind can understand (Philippians 4:7). Amen.

What worries do you have? Write them on a piece of paper. Now write "God cares" across the list. Keep the list where you can read it each time you feel worried.

Hide a Jewel

Give all your worries and cares to God, for he cares about what happens to you! (1 Peter 5:7).

Who's the Judge?

Read the Clue

Don't say, "I will get even for this wrong." Wait for the LORD to handle the matter (Proverbs 20:22).

Discover the Treasure

"Hey—where's my bike?" asked Jeff. A half hour prior, he and his stepfather had left their pickup truck in the hospital parking lot when they visited a sick friend. They'd locked Jeff's month-old mountain bike in the back of the vehicle. But now, as the duo approached the truck, the bike was nowhere to be seen.

"Someone stole it—in broad daylight!" Panic mixed with anger tinged Jeff's voice. "Who would do such a thing? I want to find the thief and punch his lights out."

"Calm down, Jeff. We'll report it to the police," said his stepfather. The two climbed into the truck and drove to the police station, where they filed a report.

"We'll do our best to find it, but chances are slim," said the police officer. "Several bikes are stolen every week in this city. The thieves take them to other cities and sell them there."

Jeff's thoughts whirled: *I worked hard for that bike. I delivered newspapers for two years. I mowed lawns. I saved my allowance. That bike means everything to me. The jerk who stole it won't get away with this.*

The officer interrupted Jeff's thoughts. "I'm sorry this happened. We'll phone if we find it."

Jeff and his stepdad thanked the officer and returned to their truck. "I don't understand why some people think it's okay to steal other people's stuff," muttered Jeff as he climbed into the cab. He pounded the seat with his fist.

"I understand your frustration, son," said Jeff's stepdad. "You worked hard and earned that bike honestly. It was the reward for your effort and sweat for the past two years. The bike means nothing but easy cash for the thief."

Jeff slouched and sneered. "It's not fair. Thanks to a common criminal, I'm minus my bike. I just want revenge."

"In a way, I don't blame you. I might feel the same way." Jeff's stepdad turned the key in the ignition and the truck's motor roared to life. "Revenge, however, won't bring your bike back. It never fixes a bad situation."

"But it might make me feel better if I could give the thief what he deserves."

"Giving the thief what he deserves is not your job," said his stepdad. He steered the truck from the parking lot onto a main road and headed for home.

"So what am I supposed to do?"

"For starters, pray that God will help the police locate your bike. Then let Him take care of the situation. The Bible calls God a fair judge and says He is angry with the wicked every day (Psalm 7:11). God passes out penalties for breaking His law in the same way a judge in an earthly court declares punishment for breaking the law. Whoever stole your bike broke God's law, and God is his fair judge. You are not. Does that make sense?"

Jeff nodded. "I think I understand. If I paid back evil for evil, I'd be breaking God's law too, right?"

"Right. God wants us to be free from evil of every sort. That's why He says to leave revenge to Him. He knows how to deal with wrongdoings in a just and fair way."

"Thanks, Dad," said Jeff. His scowl slowly melted away.

Have you ever felt like getting even with someone who hurt you or stole from you? If so, you're not alone! Many other people, including me, have felt the same way. That, however, doesn't make revenge right.

The Bible tells us God's thoughts about revenge: "See that no one pays back evil for evil. Always try to do good to each other" (1 Thessalonians 5:15). In other words, if someone does something wrong to us, we're not to punch his lights out or repay him with evil. God knows what's best for him, remember? God is the fair judge, and He knows how to deal with people who hurt us.

Share the Wealth

Dear God, we praise You because You are the fair judge (Psalm 7:11). You know everything about peoples' hearts and why they choose to do wrong things. Help us not return evil for evil, but to overcome evil with good (Romans 12:21). Amen.

When Jesus walked on the earth, did He seek revenge on people who hurt Him? Of course not! Read Luke 23:34: "Jesus said, 'Father, forgive these people, because they don't know what they are doing.'" What did Jesus do instead of punching out someone's lights? Look up 1 Peter 2:23 to see what else Jesus did.

Hide a Jewel

Never pay back evil for evil to anyone. Do things in such a way that everyone can see you are honorable (Romans 12:17).

Joseph's Story

Read the Clue

And we know that God causes everything to work together for the good of those who love God and are called according to his purpose for them (Romans 8:28).

Discover the Treasure

Sometimes bad things happen to us. A person tells a lie about us or blames us for something we didn't do. We might get hurt in an accident, or someone we love could be injured. When bad things happen, we can let circumstances make us feel angry or sorry for ourselves, or we can choose to believe that God is in control of our lives and that He can use the bad things to bring about something good and beautiful.

Joseph knows all about that. Remember him? We read his story in the book of Genesis...

"What are you guys doing? Wait a minute! Stop!" cried 17-year-old Joseph as his older brothers lunged at him. "Don't hurt me!"

Two brothers held Joseph's feet. Two more held his arms, and a fourth stripped off his new coat, a recent gift from his dad. "You're just a spoiled brat, Joseph!" they said. "Dad loves you more than he loves us. You're always tattling on us. And you act as though you're going to be our king someday. We're tired of your attitude. It's payback time!"

Joseph thrashed as his brothers carried him toward a big pit. "Please don't throw me in," he begged.

His brothers ignored his pleas. "One…two….three," said one. The brothers released their grip. Joseph landed with a thud at the bottom of the pit. "Good riddance," they joked as they sat down to eat their lunch. That's when they spied a camel caravan in the distance.

Before the day ended, they sold Joseph into slavery for 20 pieces of silver. They watched and snickered as his owners hoisted him onto a camel's back for the journey to Egypt. Was God in control? Absolutely.

Potiphar, the captain of the palace guard, purchased Joseph when he arrived in the new land. He placed the young man in charge of everything he owned. Joseph's life went well until the day Potiphar's wife told a lie about him. Potiphar believed the lie, grew furious with Joseph, and threw him into prison.

First the pit, and then the prison. Those events were bad enough, but Joseph's misadventures continued. While in jail, he interpreted dreams for two men. "When you're released, please do me a favor," he told one. "Ask Pharaoh to release me, okay?" The man was set free but unfortunately forgot about Joseph. Things looked grim for poor Joseph. But God was still in control.

Two years later, Pharaoh wanted a dream interpreted. Joseph got the job. Pharaoh was so impressed that he put Joseph in charge of all of Egypt. He dressed him in fancy clothes, placed the royal gold chain around his neck, and gave him his own signet ring to prove his authority.

God gave Joseph a plan to save the Egyptians from an upcoming famine. The plan worked so well that it provided enough food for people from surrounding lands too. And what do you think happened? Joseph's brothers showed up!

Joseph recognized his brothers immediately even though nearly 20 years had passed since they'd bullied him. As a big boss in Egypt now, he could seek revenge. Instead, he treated them with kindness and supplied them with food for their wives and children. When his brothers discovered his true identity, they were afraid he might hurt them. But Joseph wept for joy and said, "God has sent me here to keep you and your families alive so that you will become a great nation. Yes, it was God who sent me here, not you!"(Genesis 45:7-8).

The Bible doesn't tell us how Joseph felt when his brothers threw him into a pit and sold him into slavery, when Potiphar's wife lied about him and her husband threw him into prison, or when his fellow prisoner forgot about him. But it *does* tell us that God was with him during those difficult days (Genesis 39:3,21,23). He was in control the whole time. And we know that He used the bad to bring good—He saved a lot of people from starving and reunited Joseph with his family.

God is the same today. He's still in control. When you face a scary situation, remember Joseph's life and how God used the bad things to bring good. He'll do the same for you!

Share the Wealth

> Dear God, we praise You because Your thoughts are completely different from ours. Your ways are far beyond anything we can imagine (Isaiah 55:8). When bad things happen to us, help us remember that You're in control and that You can use them to bring good. Amen.

Recall a situation that seemed bad when it happened. How did God turn it into something good?

Hide a Jewel

> *Let the heavens be glad, and let the earth rejoice! Tell all the nations that the LORD is king* (1 Chronicles 16:31).

Horoscopes or God?

Read the Clue

The steps of the godly are directed by the LORD. He delights in every detail of their lives (Psalm 37:23).

Discover the Treasure

"I'm ready to sleep. How about you?" Shawna yawned and stretched her arms. It was Friday night, and several of her girlfriends had gathered at her home for a pajama party. They'd enjoyed playing card games. They'd munched popcorn while watching a movie. But midnight had passed long ago, and the party was winding down.

The girls spread their sleeping bags across the family room floor and crawled in. Shawna turned off the light. "Good night, everyone," she said. "Good night," four voices echoed.

Silence reigned for about two minutes. Then a girl named Vicki whispered, "Do you believe in horoscopes?"

"In *what?*" asked one.

"Horoscopes. You know, telling the future according to the stars."

"How's that possible? Who can tell the future according to the stars?" asked another.

"Astrologers do. They study charts that show how the stars and planets line up on certain days. They say everyone on earth was born under a certain sign like Cancer or Capricorn, and that tells our future."

"You mean the type of breakfast we'll eat in the morning is determined by the stars' position tonight?" said one girl. The others giggled.

"Don't mock," said Vicki. "I mean, the stars' position determines whether or not we'll be rich. Or famous. Or live a long life. Or be happy. In fact, an astrologer writes a daily column in the newspaper. He gives tips about how to live and what to expect every day."

Shawna had listened in silence trying to understand her friend's view, but the last sentences drew a protest. "Be careful, Vicki. An astrologer is only a person, and people don't know everything. What if he misread the chart and gave lousy advice?"

"That would never happen," said Vicki.

"It might. He's just a human, and humans make mistakes. Wouldn't it be better to trust God? After all, He knows everything about everything from history and the future."

"You sound as though you really believe that religious stuff," said Vicki.

"I do," said Shawna. "I believe God controls my life. The stars' position has nothing to do with whether or not I'll be happy or rich or whatever."

"How can you be so sure?"

"Because God's Word says so. It says God Himself has plans for us (Jeremiah 29:11). It also says God saw us before we were born. Every day of our lives is recorded in His book. Every moment was laid out before we'd lived a single day (Psalm 139:16). Does that sound as though the stars' position determines our destiny?"

"No," said Vicki. She hesitated for a moment and then quietly asked, "You sound so sure about God being in control. And if He really is as great as you say He is, I would rather believe Him than a horoscope or astrologer." She yawned and then added, "I'd like to talk more about this in the morning, okay?"

What do you think? Does our future depend on the position of the stars and planets and on an astrologer's predictions, or is God in control of what happens to us? When we look into the Bible, we find the answer to that question: God's in control.

The Bible contains lots of examples that show His control over His people's lives. Take the story of Esther, for example. Her beauty gained her the position of queen. Later, when a powerful man plotted to kill the Jews in her land, Esther used her role as queen and her position as a Jew to plead on their behalf. A lot of amazing circumstances happened that allowed Esther to save the entire nation!

Could a horoscope have determined Esther's life? Could the stars' position have worked her circumstances together to save the Jews? No. But God could.

God has a purpose for our lives. He also has the power to make that purpose come true. He's in control of our circumstances and cares about all the details of our lives—the little ones and the big ones. Because He's all-powerful and all wise, we can trust Him rather than the stars He created to direct our steps.

Share the Wealth

Dear Father, we praise You for directing our steps (Psalm 37:23). Thank You for having good plans for us (Jeremiah 29:11). We trust You to order our present and our future. Amen.

Parents, tell your children about a time when you could see that God was obviously in control of your lives.

Hide a Jewel

We can make our plans, but the LORD *determines our steps* (Proverbs 16:9).

Nothing's Impossible

Humanly speaking, it is impossible. But not with God.
Everything is possible with God (Mark 10:27).

Discover the Treasure

"I wish you wouldn't go the party tonight," said my mother. "The weather forecast says a blizzard is blowing our way."

"Don't worry, Mom," I said. "Everything will be fine. The weather forecast is probably wrong. It wouldn't be the first time."

It was December 30. I'd been invited to a year-end party at a friend's house. I'd looked forward to it for several days. Even the prospect of a blizzard couldn't dampen my excitement.

Fluffy snowflakes fell and dusted the road as Dad drove me to my girlfriend's home several blocks away. "Phone me when the party ends," he said as I climbed from the car. "I'll pick you up. Don't try walking home tonight, especially if the storm arrives."

"Sure thing," I said. "See ya later!"

The blizzard blew into town an hour later. Throughout the evening, between games and snacks, my friends and I sneaked peeks through the curtains. Soon a white blanket concealed the green lawn. It extended like a glistening quilt across the sidewalk and road. Before long, swirling snow blocked our view of the houses across the street.

The phone rang before the party ended. It was my dad. "I'm coming to get you," he said. "I'll be there in a few minutes." I slipped into my winter coat and boots and waited by the door.

A few minutes turned into a half hour. Then an hour. The storm's intensity continued to grow. *What's taking Dad so long?* I wondered. *Has he been in an accident? Is his car stuck in a snowdrift?* Finally, headlights shone through the blizzard's blinding white wall. I said goodbye to my friends and tromped through the snow to reach the car. When I opened the door, I realized my dad was not alone—he'd brought my older sister and her boyfriend. That was a smart decision.

The ride home was anything but fun. The car lurched through tire-deep drifts. When it got stuck, we three passengers climbed out, shoveled snow from the tires, and pushed. Finally the snow drifts grew impassable. The car refused to budge.

It was nearly midnight. Humanly speaking, with no help in sight and no such thing as cell phones, our situation looked impossible.

"You stay here," Dad instructed. "I'll walk home and fetch my heavy truck."

The situation grew more tense.

"I don't think that's a good idea, Dad," I said. "It's so cold. You could freeze before you reach home." I knew he suffered from a sore hip; walking in knee-deep snow for several blocks could increase his pain. My sister and her boyfriend echoed my fears, but it was no use. Dad had made his decision. He climbed from the car and began his trek.

"He'll never make it," said my sister.

"Let's pray for a miracle," said her boyfriend. And pray we did.

Within seconds, a snowmobile appeared out of nowhere and caught Dad in its headlights. The driver steered his machine in his direction. We watched in amazement as Dad climbed on the back and zoomed away.

A half hour later, we saw Dad's heavy truck plowing through the drifts. We abandoned the car and climbed into the warm truck. Within another half hour, we were sipping steamy hot chocolate at home, recalling the adventure and giving thanks to God for answering our prayers in an impossible situation.

Recalling that night still makes me shiver! Arriving home safely seemed like an impossibility. Our car was stuck in the snow. The temperatures were dangerously cold. My dad had a sore hip, which made even normal walking difficult. We had no cell phone, and there was no help in sight. But God heard our prayers and rushed to our rescue. Nothing is impossible for Him.

If you haven't already, someday you might face a situation that seems impossible. When that happens, remember—God is more powerful than anything or anyone in the universe. In fact, He created the universe! He holds the sun and stars in place. He sets the boundaries for the oceans and fills them with every type of fish and mammal imaginable. He made the earth and everything in it, including you and me.

Yes, He's a powerful God. And the best part is that this powerful God loves you and me. When we're scared, He wants us to call for help. We don't have to use fancy words or long prayers. We can simply say, "God, this looks impossible to us. But because Your Word says nothing is impossible for You, we're asking for Your help!"

Watch. He'll answer.

Share the Wealth

Dear Lord, have mercy on us. We look to You for protection. When we face situations that are difficult and seem impossible to solve, teach us to hide beneath the shadow of Your wings until the storm is past. Thank You for promising to send Your unfailing love and faithfulness from heaven to save us (Psalm 57:1-3). Amen.

Parents, tell your kids about a situation in your lives that seemed impossible. Recall how God answered your prayers for help.

Hide a Jewel

I will cry to God Most High, to God who accomplishes all things for me (Psalms 57:2 NASB).

Turtle Talk

Read the Clue

The LORD has made the heavens his throne; from there he rules over everything (Psalm 103:19).

Discover the Treasure

"Can we leave now, Mom? Please?" My third grader, Stephanie, pulled on her jacket as I finished vacuuming the floor. "Scooter's waiting. We need to pick him up."

It was March 19—a very special day. Stephanie's birthday, to be exact. She'd waited a long time for this morning, and for good reason. Several weeks prior she'd asked us to buy a box turtle for her birthday gift. I'd visited a local pet store, selected and paid for a little green fellow, and left him there for safekeeping until the big day.

A glance at the kitchen clock told me the store would be open. "Yes, it's time to bring Scooter home," I said.

"Yippee!" Stephanie shouted. She called her siblings and urged them to put on their coats. The three piled into our car, and we were off.

Twenty minutes later, we entered the store and hustled toward the turtle collection. We searched for the glass tank labeled "box turtle on hold" but found nothing. We searched again. Still nothing. We

209

expanded our search—perhaps the store staff had moved it to a different location. Nothing.

"Where is he, Mom?" said Stephanie. "Maybe they sold him to someone else. Maybe he...maybe he died." Her chin quivered and her eyes filled with tears.

I shot a quick prayer heavenward. "I'm sure there's an explanation," I said. "I'll ask a clerk to find Scooter."

Several minutes and a phone call later, the clerk returned empty-handed. "I'm very sorry," he said. "Your turtle has an eye infection. The store manager took him home so he wouldn't spread germs to the other turtles."

Stephanie's face fell. Tears spilled down her cheeks.

"Oh dear," said the worker. "I don't like to see little girls cry, especially on their birthday. Wait here—I have an idea." He disappeared into a back room, and then returned wearing a broad smile. He squatted and looked into Stephanie's sorrowful face.

"I have a special surprise for you. I'd like to give you a different turtle—a Russian tortoise. He's stronger and requires less care than a box turtle. Would you like that?" Stephanie nodded. The clerk cast me a triumphant smile. "Actually, the Russian tortoise is worth 80 dollars. The box turtle is worth only 25. I'll give you the tortoise for the same price so the birthday girl can take her present home."

I smiled back. "It's a deal."

With turtle and tank in hand, we climbed into our car and drove home. Children's chatter filled the vehicle. "Mom, I wanted a box turtle for so long," said Stephanie. "I still don't have one, but that's okay. I have a Russian tortoise instead, and he'll be easier to care for. I'm happy."

"That's a good attitude," I said.

Stephanie grinned. "This is my best birthday ever!"

Stephanie had set her heart on owning a box turtle, but things didn't happen the way she'd hoped. Has something similar ever happened to you?

Maybe you and a friend made plans to attend summer camp together, but when you arrived, you found that you were placed in different tents or cabins for the week. Perhaps you saved your money for a specific toy or pretty outfit, but when you went to the store to buy it, it was gone. Maybe you trained for running a race, but on the morning of the race, you woke up with the stomach flu and couldn't participate.

When our plans don't work out as we hope, we often feel sad or disappointed. But God's Word reminds us that He's in control of everything that happens to us. Nothing takes Him by surprise. We can trust Him because He loves us and because He knows what's good and what's not so good for us.

The next time your plans don't happen as you wish, whisper a little prayer. Say, "Thank You, God, for being in control of everything that happens in my life. Help me trust You, and help me have a good attitude even if things don't turn out the way I think they should. Amen."

Share the Wealth

> Dear God, thank You for reminding us that Your ways are far beyond anything we can imagine (Isaiah 55:8). When life doesn't happen the way we think it ought, please help us to trust You and be happy. Amen.

Have you ever faced a disappointment because your plans didn't turn out as you'd hoped? If so, how did your situation work out in the end?

Hide a Jewel

> *"My thoughts are completely different from yours," says the* LORD. *"And my ways are far beyond anything you could imagine. For just as the heavens are higher than the earth, so are my ways higher than your ways and my thoughts higher than your thoughts"* (Isaiah 55:8-9).

Scary Giants

Be strong and courageous! Do not be afraid of them! The LORD your God will go ahead of you. He will neither fail you nor forsake you (Deuteronomy 31:6).

Discover the Treasure

Have you ever faced a giant—a scary situation or a problem that seemed way too big for you to handle? If so, you're not alone.

Giants come in different shapes and sizes. Some kids describe their giant as the homework they don't understand. Others say it's meeting new friends after moving to a different city. Or dealing with their parents' divorce. Or not knowing what to do when someone hurts them and threatens to harm them again if they ask someone for help.

Giants, regardless of their shape or size, can be scary. I know. Each time I encounter one, my heart pounds like a jackhammer inside my chest. My hands grow sweaty. My knees feel like jelly powder, and my mouth goes dry.

That's how the Israelites felt when they faced Goliath, a real-life giant who seemed way too big for them to handle. And for good reason. The brute measured over nine feet tall. He wore a bronze helmet and armor that weighed 125 pounds. He carried a bronze javelin and a spear tipped with an iron head that weighed 15 pounds.

An armor bearer walked before him carrying a huge shield (1 Samuel 17:4-11,16).

For more than a month, the Israelites' army had camped across a valley from Goliath's army. And twice a day for 40 days, Goliath faced the Israelites and bellowed at them. "Send a man to fight me! If he kills me, my people will be your slaves, but if I kill him, you will be our slaves. C'mon, punks! Let's fight!"

The Israelites cowered and ran for cover. But David was different from the rest; he showed courage. One day when he delivered lunch to his soldier-brothers, he heard Goliath's shouts and saw the Israelites shake in fear. "Who is this guy anyway?" he asked. "And what right does he have to scare God's people? Give me a chance—I'll fight him!"

"You're just a kid, David," said his older brother. "You don't know what you're talking about. Go home."

The Israelite king also doubted David's ability. "Don't be ridiculous," he said. "He's too big for you."

Other youngsters might have felt discouraged and gone home. But not David. He told the king that God had enabled him to kill lions and bears with his bare hands. "He'll help me do the same to this Philistine giant," he said. Armed with only five smooth stones and a sling, he accepted Goliath's challenge to fight. He took aim, fired, and hit his target in the forehead. And that was the end of the big scary giant.

Everyone else thought the problem was way too big to handle. Everyone, that is, except David, the youngest and the smallest. Hurray for him! What made him so courageous when Goliath's presence frightened an entire army of grown men?

His faith in God.

"I come to you in the name of the LORD Almighty..." David shouted at Goliath before he charged. "The LORD does not need weapons to rescue his people. It is his battle, not ours. The LORD will give you to us!" (1 Samuel 17:45,47).

David displayed an amazing understanding of God's ability to help him fight the giant. He trusted Him, and God gave him the victory. Next time you fight a giant, whether it's a problem that seems too big to handle or a person who's giving you a hard time, use David's attitude as your example. Tell God that the battle is His and that you believe He'll rescue you. Then watch Him answer!

Share the Wealth

> Dear God, thank You for fighting our giants for us. Thank You for promising to go before us and to never leave us (Deuteronomy 31:6). Remind us of Your promises and give us courage when we face scary giants. Amen.

Take turns telling stories about giants you've faced. How did God help you fight them and win?

Hide a Jewel

> *Though a mighty army surrounds me, my heart will know no fear. Even if they attack me, I remain confident* (Psalm 27:3).

Pray, Pray, Pray

Read the Clue

Keep on asking, and you will be given what you ask for.
Keep on looking, and you will find. Keep on knocking,
and the door will be opened. For everyone who asks, receives. Everyone who seeks, finds. And the door is opened
to everyone who knocks (Matthew 7:7-8).

Discover the Treasure

Gordon's mom prayed with him every night before he fell asleep.
And every night he heard her repeat the same words: "Dear God,
please change Eddie's heart and bring him home soon. Amen."

Eddie was Gordon's 18-year-old brother. Two years prior, he'd
started hanging out with the wrong crowd at school. He became
hooked on wild parties and alcohol and drugs. His parents warned
and disciplined him, but he refused to listen and obey. One day Eddie
decided to leave home. He stuffed some clothes in a backpack, bid his
family goodbye, and walked away without a backward glance or a word
about his destination.

The boy's parents were heartbroken. They loved Eddie deeply and
felt anxious about his safety. Not a day passed without them wonder-
ing, *Where is he? What is he eating? What is he doing? Who is he with?*

And not an evening passed without his mother asking God to change his heart and bring him home soon.

With no answer to his mother's prayer in sight, Gordon grew frustrated. "It's not working, Mom," he said following her amen.

"What's not working?" she asked, still kneeling beside his bed.

Gordon rolled onto his side and looked into his mother's eyes. "Your prayer. You keep asking God to bring Eddie home, but nothing's happening. We don't even know where he is. Maybe you should quit bothering God."

His mom smiled, but her eyes looked sad. "I understand why you feel as though my prayers aren't working. You've heard me ask the same request over and over, but we haven't seen an answer yet. Sometimes I feel discouraged too. But I promise you one thing—I'll never quit praying for your brother's heart to change and for him to come home."

"Why not?" said Gordon.

"Because God's Word tells me never to give up," his mom said. "Jesus told His disciples about an old widow who'd been treated unfairly. She visited an uncaring judge and pleaded with him for justice, but he ignored her for a long time. Finally he said, 'I don't love God, and I don't care about people, but I'm going to answer her request for justice simply because she's driving me crazy. She's wearing me out with her constant requests!' (see Luke 18:2-5).

"I don't understand why it's taking so long for my prayers to be answered. But I'll follow the old woman's example. She didn't give up. She kept asking and asking until the judge finally answered. That's what I'm doing."

"So you're an old woman too?" said Gordon. He flashed a mischievous smile and pulled his blanket over his head.

"I wouldn't say that," said his mom. Now her eyes smiled too.

Have you ever prayed about something for a long, long time without seeing an answer? I have.

More than 25 years ago I began asking God to change a particular friend's heart. Twenty-five years is a long time. Sometimes I feel like telling God to hurry up. I feel impatient, and I want the answer now, especially when I see this man make some choices that hurt him and others. Then God reminds me of the old widow.

She too may have felt impatient or frustrated. She was simply asking the judge to do his job; why didn't he hop to it and grant her request? Rather than give up in despair when her requests went unanswered, however, the woman persisted. "Help me," she cried day after day. "Do justice on my behalf. Please answer me." Finally her persistence paid off. The judge granted her request, and justice was served.

Sometimes God answers our prayers immediately. Sometimes He waits a long time. We don't always understand the reason for this, but we shouldn't let it discourage us. Instead, let's do as Jesus taught—pray constantly and never give up.

Share the Wealth

Dear God, thank You for telling us to pray and for encouraging us never to give up (Luke 18:1). Thank You that Your way is perfect, and all Your promises prove true (Psalm 18:30). We know we can trust You to answer in Your way and in Your time. Amen.

Parents, tell your children about a prayer you prayed that went unanswered for a long time. How did God finally answer? What lessons did you learn through that time?

Hide a Jewel

Keep on praying (1 Thessalonians 5:17).

DeeDee's Wish List

Read the Clue

And we can be confident that he will listen to us whenever we ask him for anything in line with his will. And if we know he is listening when we make our requests, we can be sure that he will give us what we ask for (1 John 5:14-15).

Discover the Treasure

"It's bedtime. Put on your pajamas and brush your teeth," said Mrs. Thomas to her daughter DeeDee. "I'll pray with you when you're ready."

"Sure, Mom. No problem." DeeDee closed her book and dashed from the living room.

That's odd, thought Mrs. Thomas. *She usually asks permission to finish the chapter she's reading. Maybe she's just extra tired tonight, like me.* Thinking she had at least five minutes to rest, she placed her head on a cushion and closed her eyes. Less than a half minute passed before she heard her daughter's voice.

"Mom—I'm ready!"

Something's up, thought Mrs. Thomas. *This behavior isn't normal for my dawdling darling.*

"Hurry, Mom. Let's pray, okay?" said DeeDee as her mom entered the room.

"You seem so eager," said Mrs. Thomas as she sat down on the edge of DeeDee's bed. She'd barely folded her hands and closed her eyes when her daughter began.

"Dear God, please give me a white puppy and a trampoline," said DeeDee. "And I want a baby brother and a new red bike. Let's see… what else do I want? Oh yes, please give me a TV for my room and three new video games and a horse. Amen."

Mrs. Thomas stifled her laughter. "That's it?" she said.

"That's it for tonight," said DeeDee. "I'll ask for more stuff tomorrow." She crawled under her blanket and pulled it to her chin.

"Hmmm. Since when have your prayers become a list of wants?" said Mrs. Thomas.

"Since the pastor said God will give us anything we ask for. Isn't that cool?"

A puzzled expression crossed Mrs. Thomas' face. "When did the pastor say that?"

"Last Sunday. You were there, remember?"

Mrs. Thomas scratched her head. Suddenly her eyes lit up and a slow smile spread across her face. "Oh—*now* I know what you're talking about! The pastor *did* say that God will give us anything we ask for, but there's one condition: Our requests must be in line with His will."

DeeDee looked confused. "What do you mean? He won't give me a horse or a white puppy or anything else I want unless He feels like it?"

"God gives His children those things He knows are best for them," said Mrs. Thomas. "If you ask Him for a horse and He wants you to have one, He'll send it. Thankfully He doesn't give us everything we ask for. Sometimes we ask for things that we don't realize could hurt us, and then He says no."

"I'm not sure I like that," said DeeDee.

"Guess what? Even grown-ups don't always like having God say no. But we know He loves us very much and wants our best, so we can trust His answer to our prayers. Right?"

"Right," said DeeDee. "So—He might not give me a horse. But I hope He says yes to a baby brother!"

Mrs. Thomas smiled again and turned off the light. "Good night, dear DeeDee."

Some people treat God like a Santa Claus. They think He'll grant every desire on their wish list. But as Mrs. Thomas said, God doesn't give us everything we ask for. That's a good thing! If He did, our desires could prove bad for us.

To show you what I mean, I want you to think of a four-year-old child. Pretend he wants chocolate ice cream for breakfast, lunch, and supper. What might happen if he asks his mom or dad, and they agree? Before long his teeth will rot, and his body will grow weak for lack of vegetables and fruit. Saying yes to his request would be bad for his health.

If his parents are wise and truly love their son, they'll say no to three ice cream meals per day. Their decision shows that they care about his well-being. If, however, he asks for veggies and fruit three times a day, they will likely say yes because that's good nutrition and in line with their desire for his health.

Sometimes, like a good Father, God answers our requests with no, sometimes with yes. And because He loves us so much, we can trust Him all the time.

Share the Wealth

> Dear God, thank You for promising not to withhold any good thing from those who do what is right (Psalm 84:11). You are wise, and You know what's best for us. Help us to be content whether You answer our prayers with a yes or a no. Amen.

Recall a situation when God answered your prayers with a no. Did you understand the reason at the time? Did you understand it later? If so, why did He say no?

Hide a Jewel

> For the LORD God is our light and protector. He gives us grace and glory. No good thing will the LORD withhold from those who do what is right (Psalm 84:11).

Anytime, Anywhere

So wherever you assemble, I want men to pray with holy hands lifted up to God, free from anger and controversy (1 Timothy 2:8).

Discover the Treasure

Andrew was walking past his older sister's bedroom door when he heard it: "I'm so glad you're with me."

Who's with Carmen? Andrew wondered. *She's not allowed to invite friends over when Mom and Dad aren't home. She's in big trouble now.* Like a curious cat, he pressed his ear to the door.

"I'm glad you're with me everywhere I go."

Andrew's jaw dropped. *That's weird. Someone's with her everywhere she goes, and she likes that? Humph. She never lets me hang out with her.*

"You're my best friend. I'm glad I can tell you all my secrets."

Who is this dude? Andrew could stand the mystery no longer. He dropped to his knees and pressed his face to the floor, trying to sneak a peek under the door. And that's where Carmen found him when she opened the door that same instant.

"What are you doing?" she demanded.

221

"What are *you* doing?" Andrew retorted. "You're hiding someone, aren't you? Where is he? In the closet? Huh? Under the bed, maybe?"

Carmen stared at her little brother as though he'd suddenly gone crazy. "What's your problem?" She placed the palm of her hand on his forehead. "You must be delirious. Perhaps you have a fever," she said half-joking.

Ignoring his sister's comment, Andrew brushed her hand away. "I heard you talking to someone," he said. "You're not allowed to have friends over when Mom and Dad aren't here. Remember?"

"Friends?" A puzzled look crossed Carmen's face. Suddenly she burst into laughter. "Friends! Oh—I get it! Did you hear me talking to someone?"

Andrew put his hands on his hips and cocked his head. "Yes. Your best friend. Someone who knows all your secrets and is with you wherever you go."

Carmen tousled Andrew's hair and laughed again. "That's true. But it's not what you think, kiddo. I was talking to God! You know—praying."

"Praying? In the middle of the afternoon? You're kidding. I thought you only prayed before meals or at bedtime or on Sunday morning in church."

"Heavens, no," said Carmen. "It sounds like we're due for a little chat." She stepped aside and motioned for Andrew to enter her room and sit on her bed. "Like you, I used to think that people prayed only before meals or at bedtime or in church, or when they were scared about something," she admitted. "Actually, that's probably true for some folks. But I know better now.

"A few months ago, the youth pastor explained that prayer is just talking with God. He challenged us to start doing it anytime, anywhere. Now I pray when I jog and ride my bike. I chat with Him in the morning when I'm in the shower and when I'm packing my lunch for school. I talk with Him when I'm in bed at night as I'm falling asleep. The pastor was right—anytime, anywhere. It's very cool. It reminds me that God is with me 24/7. You ought to try it."

A smile played on Andrew's mouth. "Can I pray when I'm at a baseball game?"

"Sure."
"When I'm camping?"
"Of course."
"When I'm at a friend's house?"
"Absolutely. Always remember the two key words..."
"I know, I know," interrupted Andrew. *"Anytime, anywhere."*

Because God's presence is always with His children (Hebrews 13:5), we can talk with Him anytime and anywhere. Imagine what life would be like if God posted office hours: "Available to hear your prayers Monday thru Friday, eight AM to ten PM." We'd feel shunned and lonely!

Thankfully, that's not the way God works. He loves us so much that He encourages us to pray at all times, regardless of where we are. The Bible is filled with real-life examples of people who understood this truth.

Take Jonah, for instance—he cried for help from inside a fish! (Jonah 2:1-2). Elijah wandered into the desert and sat down under a lonely tree to talk with God (1 Kings 19:4). Later he prayed while cowering in a cave (verses 9-10). Hannah sat in the tabernacle when she asked God for a baby (1 Samuel 1:9). Daniel prayed three times a day, kneeling in his room with the windows open toward Jerusalem (Daniel 6:10). Peter climbed onto a housetop to pray at noon (Acts 10:9). Jesus spoke with His Father while on a mountain (Luke 9:28), in a lonely place early in the morning (Mark 1:35), and in an olive grove late at night (Matthew 26:36).

The time and place don't matter to God. He just wants our friendship. So remember the key words—*anytime, anywhere*—and enjoy talking with Him.

Share the Wealth

Dear God, we praise You for being a God who is everywhere at all times. Even if we ride the wings of the morning and dwell by the farthest oceans, You are there (Psalm 139:9-10). Because of who You are, we have the freedom to pray anytime, anywhere. Thank You for that privilege. Amen.

Name your family's favorite places to visit. Name the places you've been in the past week, even for routine errands. Ask the children if it's possible to pray in these locations.

Hide a Jewel

I can never escape from your spirit! I can never get away from your presence! (Psalm 139:7).

Always the Same

Read the Clue

Jesus Christ is the same yesterday, today, and forever (Hebrews 13:8).

Discover the Treasure

Saturday evening was reserved for a special family activity at the Taylor house. Tonight was no exception. Mom popped popcorn and prepared hot chocolate while Dad set up an ancient projector in the living room. "It's ready!" he called. "Roll 'em!"

The two Taylor kids dashed into the room and plopped on the couch. Mom served the popcorn and Dad dimmed the lights. "I hope you enjoy these old movies," he said. "You'll see lots of change in the people."

The projector flashed black and white pictures on the screen. "Who's that?" said Shane, pointing at a family standing beside a well-used pickup truck. The woman held a toddler. A long, plain dress and white apron covered her slender figure. Her husband wore coveralls and a plaid jacket.

"Grandma and Grandpa. The child is my oldest brother—your Uncle Les."

"Wow—look at his dark hair! Now he's nearly bald," said Shane. "And look at that truck—you don't see anything like that on the roads these days. Did it actually run?"

"Of course," said Dad. "Not as smooth as the pickups nowadays, but it did the job. Of course the speed limits were much slower than they are now." Scene after scene rolled past as Dad identified people and places. When the reel ended, he exchanged it for another one. "These pictures are more recent," he said. "I wonder if you'll recognize anyone."

A moment later, a young boy with curly white-blonde hair appeared on the screen. A woman set a birthday cake before him. He huffed and puffed at the three burning candles and clapped his hands in excitement when he blew out their flames. "Who do you think that is?" said Dad.

Shane's sister, Stasi, eyed her dad. His hair was brown now, but the waves were unmistakable. "You?" she asked. She burst into laughter. "You were such a cute little kid. What happened?"

Dad laughed too. He laughed more when his brother appeared in the movie sporting a brush-cut hairdo and wearing big black-rimmed glasses. His pants were three inches too short. "Meet Uncle Les in his teens," he said.

The evening ended with a video of a recent family wedding. "Grandma and Grandpa look so different," said Stasi. "In the movie, they were tall and slender and young. Now they're short and round. Their hair's white and their faces are wrinkled."

"Uncle Les got rid of his bookworm glasses and short pants, thank goodness. Now he dresses in suits and ties," observed Shane. "And look at you, Stasi. You dyed your hair for that wedding, remember? It turned orange!"

Stasi laughed at the memory. "Yeah, I'm glad it finally washed out."

"That's it for tonight's show," said Dad when the video ended. "What did you think?"

"You were right—everyone changed a lot," said Shane. "It's fun to see what people looked like 50 years ago."

"Some look totally different now," said Stasi. "That's good in some cases but not so good in others!"

"Yes, change is inevitable," said Mom. "But one person never changes—God. We grow old, but He never does. Our circumstances change. Sometimes our personalities change. But He remains the same, for which I'm very thankful."

"Me too," said Dad.

I too am thankful that God remains the same forever. What would life be like if He grew old and forgetful about fulfilling His promises to us? What if He became hard of hearing and couldn't hear our prayers? What if He changed from being present everywhere at all times to being absent sometimes? And what if He changed His rules whenever He felt like it?

If God changed as people do, we'd be in big trouble. We'd have no assurance that He would keep His promises. We'd have no guarantee that He would listen to our prayers. And we wouldn't have a clue about which rules to obey and which ones to ignore.

Thankfully, God never changes. And because that's true, we can live in peace even though everything changes around us.

Share the Wealth

> Dear God, we praise You because You are the same yesterday, today, and forever (Hebrews 13:8). You created all heaven's lights, but unlike them, You never change (James 1:17). Help us live in peace, knowing that You will always be faithful and true to Your Word and to us. Amen.

Because God never changes, His standards for our lives remain the same. Name three standards He wants for His children's behavior (for example, speaking the truth, honoring our parents, and not stealing). What would life be like if God suddenly decided those standards didn't matter anymore?

Hide a Jewel

> *Before the mountains were created, before you made the earth and the world, you are God, without beginning or end* (Psalm 90:2).

The Greatest Treasure of All

Some folks think the Bible is just a book of rules for religious people. Actually, nothing could be further from the truth. As I said in my note at the beginning of this book, it's a treasure chest filled with pearls of wisdom and gems of truth. If we practice those truths they can change our lives and give us the greatest treasure of all—eternal life.

But eternal life has one condition—we must admit our spiritual poverty by confessing our sin and acknowledging our need for a Savior. Have you done that? If not, now's the time. Here's how...

The Bible says we've all sinned and fallen short of God's standard (Romans 3:23). It also says that the wages of sin is death, but the free gift of God is eternal life through Jesus Christ our Lord (Romans 6:23). In other words, regardless of how many good deeds we do or how many citizenship awards we win, we're doomed unless we believe that Jesus Christ paid our death penalty when He died on the cross and that He purchased a place in heaven for us when He rose from the dead three days later. When we trust in Jesus to take away our sins, we're made right with God (Romans 3:22) and receive the gift of everlasting life.

I received that gift by praying a simple prayer when I was eight years old. It went like this:

Lord Jesus Christ, I know I'm a sinner and don't deserve eternal life. But I believe You died and rose from the grave to purchase a place in heaven for me. Jesus, come into my life. Take control of my life. Forgive my sins and save me. I turn from anything that is not pleasing to You and place my trust in You for salvation. I accept the free gift of eternal life. Amen.

Praying this prayer didn't make my life problem free, but it guaranteed an eternal relationship with the One who loves me unconditionally and created me for a purpose. The same is true for you if you've asked Jesus to be your Savior.

If you invited Christ to come into your life, I'd love to offer encouragement. Please feel free to contact me through my website: www.gracefox.com.

Know you are loved,

Grace

Other Great Harvest House Books
by Grace Fox

10-Minute Time Outs for Moms

Insightful devotions from author and mother Grace Fox empower you to maintain a vital connection with God. Inspiring stories, Scripture-based prayers, and practical guidance offer you strength for your spiritual journey and daily life.

10-Minute Time Outs for Busy Women

Grace Fox encourages you to make time for what matters most—your relationship with God. Her real-life stories and Scripture-based prayers will help you understand God's truth and apply it to everyday life.

If you would like to share your story with Grace or invite her to speak to your church, women's group, conference, or retreat, visit her website at www.gracefox.com.